Coastal Walks in the
North Island

Coastal Walks in the
North Island

Marios Gavalas

NEW
HOLLAND

First published in 2004 by New Holland Publishers (NZ) Ltd
Auckland • Sydney • London • Cape Town

218 Lake Road, Northcote, Auckland, New Zealand
14 Aquatic Drive, Frenchs Forest, NSW 2086, Australia
86–88 Edgware Road, London W2 2EA, United Kingdom
80 McKenzie Street, Cape Town 8001, South Africa

www.newhollandpublishers.co.nz

Copyright © 2004 in text: Marios Gavalas
Copyright © 2004 in photography: Marios Gavalas
Copyright © 2004 New Holland Publishers (NZ) Ltd

National Library of New Zealand Cataloguing-in-Publication Data

Gavalas, Marios
Coastal walks in the North Island / Marios Gavalas.
ISBN 1-86966-071-4
1. Hiking—New Zealand—North Island—Guidebooks. 2. Shorelines—
New Zealand—North Island—Guidebooks. I. Title.
796.5209931—dc 22

Managing editor: Matt Turner
Editing and design: Alison Dench
Cover design: Gina Hochstein

10 9 8 7 6 5 4 3 2 1

Colour reproduction (cover) by Microdot, Auckland, New Zealand
Colour reproduction (internal) by Pica Digital, Singapore
Printed by Times Offset (M) Sdn Bhd, Malaysia

Contents

Introduction

The North Island boasts an unparalleled coastline, from massive dominating cliffs to tranquil beaches. Its varied and lengthy margins exhibit distinct characteristics, all with individual qualities worthy of discovery.

The coast of the northern tip of the country is characterised by long sweeping beaches on the west and a craggy meandering coast on the east. These themes are continued in the Auckland region, with the islands of the Hauraki Gulf adding another dimension. Coromandel has a necklace of golden beaches edged with verdant headlands, while the Bay of Plenty's sweeping beaches are punctuated by occasional high points and former pa sites.

The sandy coves of Eastland have misty tones and turquoise waters. Massive cliffs dominate the Hawke's Bay coast, and these continue to the Wairarapa, where the ocean's fury is played out in an exhibition of power. Around Wellington the coast is mostly rocky, contrasting with the long, broad beaches of the Wanganui coastline. Around Taranaki the low coastal relief hides some fine walks and the little-known Waikato coastline has its own delights.

An ocean vista often inspires a sense of dreaming. The beat of surf against rock, the salt-charged air, the biting wind and the unmistakable aroma of the sea combine to create an atmosphere unlike any other. The coastline draws us, energises our souls and uplifts our spirits.

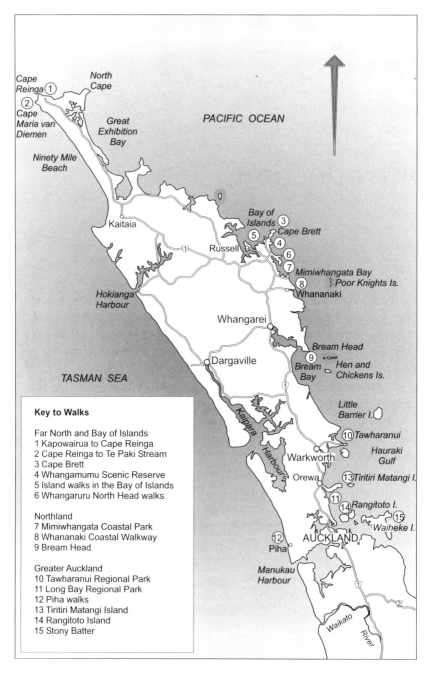

Key to Walks

Far North and Bay of Islands
1 Kapowairua to Cape Reinga
2 Cape Reinga to Te Paki Stream
3 Cape Brett
4 Whangamumu Scenic Reserve
5 Island walks in the Bay of Islands
6 Whangaruru North Head walks

Northland
7 Mimiwhangata Coastal Park
8 Whananaki Coastal Walkway
9 Bream Head

Greater Auckland
10 Tawharanui Regional Park
11 Long Bay Regional Park
12 Piha walks
13 Tiritiri Matangi Island
14 Rangitoto Island
15 Stony Batter

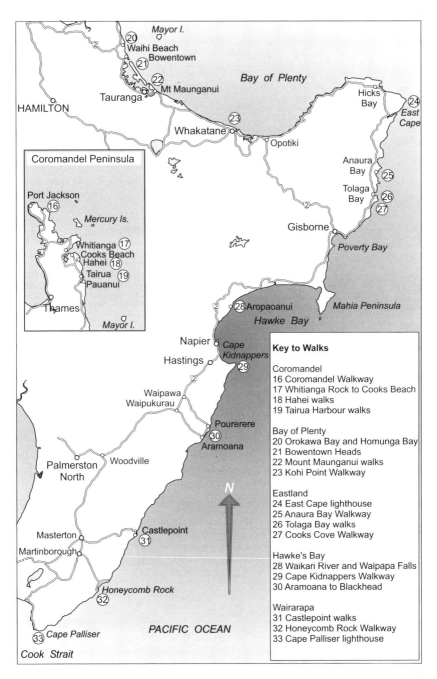

Key to Walks

Coromandel
16 Coromandel Walkway
17 Whitianga Rock to Cooks Beach
18 Hahei walks
19 Tairua Harbour walks

Bay of Plenty
20 Orokawa Bay and Homunga Bay
21 Bowentown Heads
22 Mount Maunganui walks
23 Kohi Point Walkway

Eastland
24 East Cape lighthouse
25 Anaura Bay Walkway
26 Tolaga Bay walks
27 Cooks Cove Walkway

Hawke's Bay
28 Waikari River and Waipapa Falls
29 Cape Kidnappers Walkway
30 Aramoana to Blackhead

Wairarapa
31 Castlepoint walks
32 Honeycomb Rock Walkway
33 Cape Palliser lighthouse

Coastal Walks in the North Island

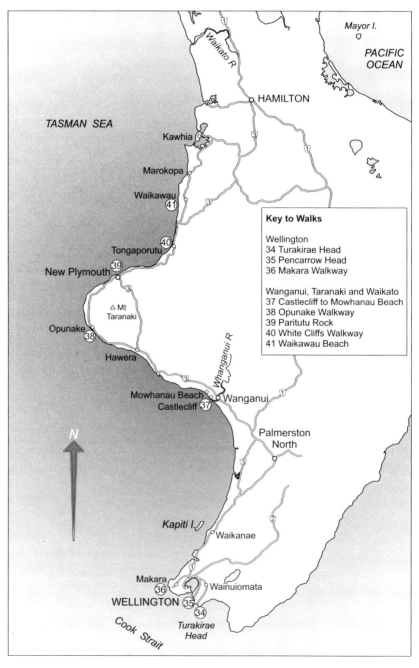

Key to Walks

Wellington
34 Turakirae Head
35 Pencarrow Head
36 Makara Walkway

Wanganui, Taranaki and Waikato
37 Castlecliff to Mowhanau Beach
38 Opunake Walkway
39 Paritutu Rock
40 White Cliffs Walkway
41 Waikawau Beach

The coastal environment

The coast is a dynamic environment, charged with the forces of nature interplaying to create the landforms explored in this book. Where land battles the sea we admire perfect crescents of sand flanked by golden dunes, sinuous estuaries with many tentacles smothered in a border of hardy vegetation, craggy headlands chiselled to bulbous shapes, and exposed rock carved into arches, stacks and reefs.

The coast is an environment of unceasing change where pounding surf grinds away at the land's edge, shaping and sculpting it into the features that attract us. Wind, salt and sun combine to weather the rock, and wave action is the main erosive agent. With each breaking wave a tumultuous force is unleashed and cobbles, pebbles and sand are catapulted at the coastal rock. The impact exploits weaknesses in the rocks, splitting them apart.

The eastern seaboard of the northern part of the North Island, with its craggy coast of headlands collapsed into saw-tooth profiles dwindling to reefs, is testimony to these processes. At Cathedral Cove a cleft in the cliff has been excavated by waves to form a massive rock arch. This will eventually collapse to form an offshore stack like Te Hoho Rock at the northern end of the beach. The final part of the process is the degradation of the stack to a low stump or reef. The composition of the rock contributes greatly to the type of features that develop.

The tension between tectonic uplift and the denuding action of waves is played out at Cape Kidnappers in Hawke's Bay. Here the sedimentary rock is periodically forced up by earth movements and is dislodged in massive blocks. The sea chisels away, causing the blocks to slump and cleave. Around the south coast near Wellington and the Wairarapa, high sea cliffs have been attacked and cloaks of gently curving scree now protect their bases. Often a narrow coastal foot skirts the margins and provides walking access.

If tectonic processes did not lift the land, then the ocean would eventually wear the coast to flat plains like those around the Bay of Plenty or Wanganui. Long beaches edged with vast dune fields, tidal flats and low-lying sandy islands are characteristic of these coasts.

Where tectonic forces pull the land down, the sea takes over, drowning river valleys and isolating beaches, creating bars across the mouths of estuaries. The Bay of Islands is a system of drowned river valleys filled in with sediment: where once there were undulating headlands, now there are islands. The sea transports sediment and deposits it where its energy dwindles. Through longshore drift, sand particles are moved along the coast, changing the profile of beaches. Once-detached islands such as Bowentown Heads in the Bay of Plenty can become reattached to the land by tombolos or sandspits, creating long, finger-like beaches.

Spray from seawater in the splash zone coats the inside of rock cracks and the expanding salt crystals force the cracks wider, preparing them for the onslaught of wave degradation. The walk to Honeycomb Rock in the Wairarapa explores the results of these processes, manifested in unusual patterns on the rock.

The coastal habitat

The flora and fauna inhabiting the land's fringe live in a hostile environment. They have to contend with tides, salt and wind, the pounding of breaking surf and heating from the intense sun. Rocky shores, sandy beaches and tidal estuaries have evolved particular communities of inhabitants, all adapted to their precarious living space.

On rocky shores the intertidal zone is a unique environment with a hardy assemblage of life organising itself according to its position in relation to the mean tide mark. The distinct zonation is determined by tolerance to sun and desiccation at the upper end, and ability to compete with other organisms lower down.

At low tide most inhabitants retreat to crevices, hollows and rock pools. The only life visible in the sea is the beds of sea kelp swaying in the current. Each rock pool supports a microcosm of sea life. Snails slither across the rocky faces grazing on microscopic plankton. Crabs and starfish emerge, and chitons cling to hollows. Periwinkles, barnacles, limpets and mussels encrust the rocks in a striking pattern. At high tide organisms emerge from their hiding places and life is played out to the full beneath the ocean surface.

Pebbled beaches, especially those around Wellington, support unusual communities of plants. A walk from Pencarrow Head along the coast to Baring Head reveals low clumps of hardy cushion plants such as *Pimelea urvilleana*. Nearby, fur seals escape temporarily from the surf to the rocks. The smell is usually the first indication of their presence. With a diet of squid and fish and an oily skin above thick layers of blubber, they have a unique odour. Seals generally use North Island rocky shores only as haul-out sites, most breeding colonies being confined to the South Island. Chance encounters with fur seals can occur on any walk south of Hawke's Bay. Should you come across a fur seal, stay on the landward side.

Sandy shores, although not supporting the same breadth of life as rocky shores, still nurture plant communities, especially on dunes. The dunes are formed by the prevailing wind, which deposits sand grains on the leeward side of an irregularity such as a rock or clump of grass. This enlarges the obstruction and starts a positive feedback process. As the dune becomes larger it will move slowly inland unless it is colonised by vegetation. Hardy plants such as the native sedge pingao *Desmoschoenus spiralis* or the native sand grass *Spinifex hirsutus* send out tentacled roots just beneath the dune surface, holding the structure together. More recently, however, introduced marram grass has displaced the natives. Once the dunes are stabilised, other drought-tolerant plants such as ice plants and groundsel take root.

Dune fields flank some beaches and come under severe pressure from coastal development. Dune systems take years to form and protect the areas behind them. They are usually protected with access ways, which should always be used to cross them.

Tidal estuaries harbour bountiful ecosystems replenished with nutrients by both land and sea. A river's load of sediment is deposited at the sea and builds up as tidal mudflats. Following colonisation by mangroves, salt marshes form, succeeded by flax, cabbage trees and other coastal forest species. Birds, including waders, graze the fertile mudflats picking at fish, gastropods and other molluscs.

These coastal communities are fragile. They should be treated with respect.

Birds of the coast

New Zealand dotterel (*Charadrius obscurus*)
The diminutive, shy New Zealand dotterel is a delicate bird with a white belly and pale brown back. Breeding plumage varies significantly. It is becoming a rarity on the beaches of the upper North Island. Predation of eggs by stoats, cats and dogs, coupled with inconsiderate use of the beaches by humans, destroys clutches of eggs laid in small depressions around dunes. Birds may fake a broken wing to discourage you from passing too close to nests.

Australasian gannet (*Sula bassana serrator*)
The sight of a gliding gannet usually comes with the expectation of a dive. Spying its prey from above, the gannet plummets towards the sea with wings notched into a V-shape. On impact with the water, its internal nostrils prevent water being forced into the nasal cavity, and air sacs inflate beneath the skin on the lower neck and breast. The gannet can hit the water at up to 145 km/h and usually swallows its prey while underwater.

The large wing-span imparts majesty in flight and the attractive golden head is accentuated by a black stripe running through each eye. The trailing edge of the wing is black. Pairs often mate for life and juveniles depart for Australia, where they spend their formative years, before returning for a life in New Zealand waters.

Variable oystercatcher (*Haematopus unicolor*)
Each variable oystercatcher displays a different white chest marking on otherwise black plumage. These birds give a high-pitched call at the slightest provocation and will often walk a considerable distance up the beach ahead of you before taking flight. They fly low, close to the water and with a powerful wing beat, and feed at the mouths of rivers and estuaries.

Caspian tern (*Hydroprogne caspia*)
The Caspian tern is distinguished from the more boisterous red-billed gull by its pointed wings and erratic wing beat. Flocks often congregate on offshore stacks or rocky outcrops, awaiting shoals of fish to feed on. Terns can dive with accomplished aerobatic skill to capture their prey.

Black-backed gull (*Larus dominicanus*)
The boisterous black-backed gull is the bully of the avian world's coastal residents. Its large physical size, screeching call and intimidating nature filter through to other birds, who react with submission and fear. Common throughout the North Island, this scavenger scours the shoreline for flotsam and jetsam and thrives in human inhabited areas, where it rips rubbish bags and spills the contents over the roadside.

Red-billed gull (*Larus novaehollandiae*)
The red-billed gull is especially abundant on the eastern coastline and is rarely seen alone. Flocks of the uniformed gulls loiter on headlands or near humans, in hope of titbits to scavenge. The bright red bill is matched with scarlet feet, which can be visibly damaged by squabbles – or close encounters with cars.

Walking on the coast

Safety

The shoreline is the first line of defence against the ocean. The power of cascading waves is absorbed by the coastal margins, clouds drop their contents on the first land they encounter, and the winds can be ferocious.

Headlands, in particular, experience concentrations of these powerful environmental forces. Wind funnels through breaks in the cliffs and accelerates over low points on headland ridges. Waves ride up cliff faces and the spray can be blinding when whipped up by the wind.

The rhythms of the tides may catch the unwary on some walks. Always check tide times before embarking on tidal walks and be conservative with estimates of what is possible in a certain time window. Never try to race the tide: the approaching ocean is unrelenting and unforgiving. Beware of freak waves on headlands and on coastal platforms. Rocky shores can be very slippery, with algal films soaked to a lethal slickness by the sea spray. Cross dunes only on the paths indicated. Where tracks cross streams or rivers, seek local advice on water levels. If it has been raining previous to, or during, your walk, streams may be high. Do not attempt to cross a stream in flood: wait until it subsides.

Always check the weather forecast before departing because

conditions can change very quickly. Take plenty of water, food and, if necessary, shelter. Make sure you are fit enough for the grade of walk you are attempting and wear strong shoes, preferably sturdy boots. Take a detailed map (e.g. 1:50,000 Topomap NZ260 Map Series) and compass if there is any uncertainty about the route.

Inform a friend, relative or Department of Conservation (DoC) visitor centre of your intended itinerary before departing on a walk. Many walks in this book pass through valleys and remote coastal areas. Repeater stations can be few and far between, so do not rely on a cellphone to call for help.

Where a track can be attempted from both directions, the descriptions given in the book apply to one direction only. If you attempt a walk in one direction only, make sure you arrange suitable transport to meet you at the walk's conclusion.

Track grades
Please note that the grades suggested in this book are subjective and are provided as a guide only. Tracks are graded according to length, gradient and surface.

Grade	Easy *Track surface is even with only minor undulations. Directions are either clearly signposted or obvious. Walk is usually short.*
Grade	Easy/Medium *Track usually involves some inclines and requires a reasonable level of fitness.*
Grade	Medium *Track surface can be uneven and the walk may involve frequent inclines. A good level of fitness is required.*
Grade	Hard *Track may be very steep and uneven. These walks are usually reserved for people with excellent fitness and some outdoor experience.*

New Zealand Environmental Care Code

When walking the North Island coast:

- Protect rare and endangered plants and animals.
- Remove rubbish. Take it away with you.
- Bury toilet waste in a shallow hole away from waterways, tracks, campsites and huts.
- Keep streams clean.
- Take care with fires. If you must build a fire, keep it small, use dead wood, and douse it with water when you leave. Before you go, remove any evidence. Portable stoves are preferable, as they are more efficient and pose less risk to the environment.
- After camping, leave the site as you found it.
- Keep to the track. This minimises the chances of treading on fragile seedlings.
- Respect the cultural heritage.
- Enjoy yourself.
- Consider others. Respect everybody's reasons for wanting to enjoy the North Island's coastal beauty.

Far North and Bay of Islands

The Far North, the last gasp of mainland New Zealand, is a unique and wild area, a landscape that boasts magnificent coastal features including the country's most extensive dune systems. Pristine beaches fringe vast wetlands that rise to hills cloaked in regenerating vegetation.

Farther south, the Bay of Islands draws throngs of tourists, who visit to appreciate the turquoise waters and sprinkling of islands. Long pre-European and European histories add interest to the walks in this majestic setting.

1

Kapowairua
to Cape Reinga

The raw isolation of Spirits Bay, the jagged coastline and the reward of Cape Reinga lighthouse are among the Cape Reinga Coastal Walkway's most memorable attributes. The arrival at Cape Reinga is made all the more satisfying having walked there and experienced some of Te Paki Recreation Reserve's invigorating majesty – and there is a sense of superiority over the tourist hordes disembarking from their vehicles.

To Maori the area around Cape Reinga is sacred. Maori believe that after travelling Te Oneroa-a-Tohe (Ninety Mile Beach), a spirit will climb Haumu, a high hill on the edge of the dunes, and pay its last respects to the world. After a final drink from the stream called Te Wai-o-ngunguru ('waters of the underworld'), the spirit passes through the exposed root of the legendary pohutukawa tree at Te Rerenga-wairua ('leaping place of the spirits', Cape Reinga). The final transition to the spirit world involves a visit to the island of Manawa Tawhi ('last breath') and thence to Hawaiki.

The complete walkway from Kapowairua to Cape Reinga is a very long day's walk, and transport must be arranged at both ends. There are no scheduled buses, boats or planes. Te Paki is very isolated and undeveloped. The challenging walk can be broken into stages (Kapowairua to Pandora, Pandora to Tapotupotu and Tapotupotu to Cape Reinga), and DoC provides campgrounds at Kapowairua (only open in summer) and Tapotupotu Bay. These have toilets and water and at Tapotupotu Bay there are cold-water showers. There is also an informal camping area at Pandora. There are toilets at Cape Reinga.

Seek advice from DoC in Kaitaia or Te Paki before starting the walk.

Kapowairua to Pandora

The eastern portion of the Cape Reinga Coastal Walkway skirts Spirits Bay, New Zealand's northernmost accessible beach.

Grade	Hard
Time	2$^1/_2$ hours one-way along beach 2 hours one-way behind dunes
Access	Spirits Bay is signposted along Te Hapua Road, 21 km before Cape Reinga. Spirits Bay Road is a further 6 km on the left. Kapowairua is at the roadend. The track starts behind the dunes and is signposted on the left just before the road ends.
Note	Pandora is the far side of the Waitahora Stream. The stream is waist deep and a crossing can be made only at low tide. Check stream levels with DoC before embarking on the walk.

The dunes to the west of the carpark shield the waiting delights of Spirits Bay. A brief excursion up the low hill above the parking area and campground at Kapowairua shows not only the way ahead, but also a 9-lb cannon formerly owned by Hongi Keepa. The Maori chief acquired it from a whaler in the early 1800s. To the west the 8-km expanse of Spirits Bay draws your attention to the ocean and distant hills. The stunning location and easy access to marine resources have made this contested territory and many human bones have been unearthed, suggesting this may have been a battleground or burial site. Captain Cook sailed past in 1769 and noted a village on the western hills

23

above the bay. Terraces and hangi pits are still visible from near Waitahora Stream. Cook didn't anchor here, unlike Marion du Fresne and his French crew in 1772. They sent reconnaissance parties ashore for fresh water and encountered a fierce storm in which one ship lost two anchors.

Two routes lead to a meeting at Waitahora Stream. In effect, Spirits Bay is a sandspit, with one track following the exposed ocean side and the other meandering beside the more sheltered wetland area behind the dunes. The sand on the beach route is soft, making progress arduous. The calf muscles especially seem to feel the strain as the coarse sand offers little resistance to each step. The route behind the dunes follows orange marker posts along a vehicle track and has a comprehensive view of the impenetrable wetlands. The still waters around the clumps of reeds and rushes are a breeding ground for mosquitoes, which reach a frightening size and swarm in large numbers in summer. By day, when the mosquitoes are asleep, the sandflies take over. Bring plenty of insect repellent, especially if camping at Kapowairua.

Pandora to Tapotupotu

The middle section of the coastal walkway starts at Pandora, a remote sandy beach reached only on foot.

Grade	Hard
Time	3^1/$_2$ hours one-way
Access	Pandora is accessible only from the coastal walkway. To reach Tapotupotu, turn right into unsealed Tapotupotu Road 2.5 km before Cape Reinga. It is 3 km along the snaking road to the bay.

The name 'Pandora' seems remarkably apt for this gem of a beach nestled in an inaccessible location. Named after HMS *Pandora*, a survey ship that visited the coast in 1849, Pandora has not always been so isolated. During the development of New Zealand's nascent tourist industry in the 1920s, a camp formerly occupied the grass clearing. The slightly eccentric proprietor, Captain Hector McQuarrie, constructed bush huts from local materials. His 'resort' appealed to the 'high society' of the day and the dance hall was reputed to have an 'excellent floor', allegedly constructed from shipwreck timber. The camp was advertised as being 'Away up where New Zealand Ends' and was frequented by the 'carriage trade' in need of rejuvenation. The tough journey up Ninety Mile Beach and over the steep hills to the camp could not have been comfortable, but the effort was rewarded with scenic beauty and solitude.

At low tide, skirt the base of the headlands by walking over the rocks. A high-tide route is signposted and marked with orange posts. It is less interesting and more arduous, traversing two headlands on a track worn through the long grass. It can be steep and muddy (45 minutes).

Head left along the vehicle track and climb to a signposted junction with Darkies Ridge (40 minutes).

From here it is 2 hours to Tapotupotu. The scenery changes little, so simply enjoy the raw feel of the place. Te Paki feels like an island, somehow detached from mainland New Zealand, and this section of the walk emphasises that. It is just your walking party and the outdoors, a fine time to reflect on life or formulate dreams. First walk along the old vehicle track then follow a grass track lined with orange posts. The track heads to a clifftop ridge and descends steeply to Tapotupotu Bay.

Tapotupotu to Cape Reinga

The dramatic sheer cliffs and the views from Cape Reinga to North Cape are the highlights of this section of the coastal walkway.

Grade	Hard
Time	1$^1/_2$ hours one-way
Access	To reach Tapotupotu, turn right into unsealed Tapotupotu Road 2.5 km before Cape Reinga. It is 3 km along the snaking road to the bay. The track starts from the western side of Tapotupotu Bay. Look for the orange rectangle on a post. If starting from Cape Reinga, the signposted track departs from the eastern side of the parking area.

For 20 minutes follow the grass track, marked with orange posts, to the ridge, where it enters low scrub for a further 20 minutes. The descent to unimaginatively named Sandy Bay is steep and takes 20 minutes. From here, it is a 30-minute steady climb to Cape Reinga. In places the track rests on the clifftop, so beware of strong wind gusts.

2

Cape Reinga
to Te Paki Stream

A glance at the map of the North Island's most northerly appendage shows the high islands around Te Paki joined to the mainland by a long finger of subdued relief. Around 5 million years ago the Aupouri Peninsula, including Te Paki, was a series of islets, an archipelago in shallow seas. Fluctuations in sea level and the transportation of huge volumes of sand caused large sandspits to form, encouraged by the prevailing south-westerly winds. Te Paki eventually joined the greater North Island landmass, but it still retains an island character. The area is an outstanding habitat for rare species of flora and fauna and the geographical isolation has led to subspecies evolving differently from their mainland counterparts.

After early European attempts to harness the land, Te Paki station was formed and originally covered a massive 40,500 ha. It was acquired by Samuel Yates, who married a local chief's daughter and was known as 'King of the North' until his death in 1900. He ran over 8000 sheep and 2000 cattle on the marginal land. Cattle from the station were usually driven down Ninety Mile Beach, the local main highway.

The station was later bought by Richard Keene, a Wellington business-man, whose family sold it to the government in 1966. The land was then leased to a company that made a misguided attempt to grow tung trees for the manufacture of tung oil. The venture was thwarted because the trees required shelter, an environmental characteristic almost entirely absent from Te Paki. A few specimens still grow in the valleys.

Walks at Te Paki often cross beaches and meander around small bays. At the ends of the bays are orange rectangles on posts, indicating where to rejoin the track. These are mostly easy to find, but some have been consumed by slips and take a little searching to find.

Grade	Hard
Time	$2^1/_4$ hours one-way to Te Werahi Gate 7 hours one-way to Te Paki Stream $8^1/_2$ hours one-way including detour to Cape Maria Van Diemen
Access	From the carpark at Cape Reinga, the start of the track to Te Werahi Beach is signposted. If starting the walk from Te Paki Stream carpark, follow Te Paki Stream Road for 4 km, 17 km before Cape Reinga. To join the walk via the Te Werahi Gate to Te Werahi Beach Track look for the signpost on the left 4.5 km before Cape Reinga. It is a 1-hour descent to join the Cape Reinga Coast Walk.
Notes	If possible, time the walk to cross Te Werahi Stream at low tide. However, a mid-tide crossing can be accomplished if stream levels permit. Beware of vehicles, which use Ninety Mile Beach and Te Paki Stream as highways. Seek advice from DoC in Kaitaia or Te Paki before embarking on the walk.

Guidebooks boast that Cape Reinga is the northerly tip of New Zealand. Although Cape Reinga is actually 3 km south of Surville Cliffs, it is the most northerly accessible point on the mainland of New Zealand. This fact is enough to encourage coachloads of tourists, who snap a photo at the concrete tower of Cape Reinga lighthouse and return to Kaitaia or the Bay of Islands.

The iconic symbol stands 10 m tall and is 165 m above sea level. The lens of the light was shipped from England and first installed in a lighthouse on Motuopao Island in 1879. Cape Reinga lighthouse started operating in 1941.

This is an awe-inspiring place to admire the ocean, which seems vast and unforgiving. Try to get here early in the morning before the tourists arrive – you may even have the place to yourself. To the west, the turbid water of Columbia Bank eddies in a deep blue swirl. It is here the calmer Pacific Ocean meets the wind-whipped waters of the Tasman Sea. The confluence of two ocean currents provides a menu of nutrients, attracting abundant marine life. To the north, the Three Kings Islands were named on the eve of the Feast of Epiphany by Abel Tasman to commemorate the magi of the New Testament.

From Cape Reinga follow the wide track down to Te Werahi Beach (30 minutes). Clumps of flax gyrate in the breeze and hazy views stretch south to the beach. The firm sand is easy walking (45 minutes) and may warrant removal of your boots.

The track to Te Werahi Gate departs from the southern end of the beach and is indicated with an orange rectangle on a post. It is 1 hour from here through paddocks, wetland and scrub to Te Werahi Gate on SH1F, 4.5 km before Cape Reinga.

If continuing south, be careful of Te Werahi Stream at the southern end of the beach, which should be crossed at low to mid tide. On the far side of the stream look for large orange triangles on posts indicating the track over Herangi Hill to the Cape Maria Van Diemen turnoff (45 minutes). The dunes around Herangi Hill are a colourful mixture of red, ochre, peach, white and golden sands. The crust of caked sand is dotted with rock, tufts of orange pingao – and snail shells. This seems a bizarre encounter in an arid landscape, but the endangered flax snail *Placostylus ambagiosus* is prevalent in the area. Unfortunately wild pigs have developed a taste for the fleshy inners of the shells and the descendants of the snails whose fossilised shells are found in the dunes near Cape Maria Van Diemen are in trouble. The only other places the species occurs are the Solomon Islands and Fiji, suggesting either the connection of these landmasses to NZ in times of lower sea level, or the snails rafting on drifting logs.

The 1¹/₂-hour detour to the cape drops down the southern side of a large sand bowl (20 minutes). In this other-worldly landscape it is easy to become mesmerised by the patterns in the sand blown by the ever-present wind. Climb the steep grass bank along a formed but unmarked track to the light station (25 minutes), a convenient place for refreshment. Cape Maria Van Diemen was named by Abel Tasman on 5 January 1643 to honour the wife of the governor-general of Batavia. Had the explorer made landfall, he probably would not have ventured too far inland, such is the harshness of the place. Return to the main track by the same route.

It is a further 45 minutes along an old vehicle track through low vegetation to the north-western end of Twilight Beach (Te Paengarehia), which takes 40 minutes to walk. Twilight Beach was named after the schooner *Twilight*, wrecked on 25 March 1871 with the loss of two lives. More disastrously, in 1966 the collier *Kaitawa* sank nearby in rough seas and all 29 crew members died. The wheelhouse, doors from the superstructure and lifebuoys were later washed ashore and opportunists managed to salvage some of the wreckage.

At the south-eastern end of the beach an old vehicle track crosses Scott Point through low vegetation (1½ hours). The thin peat soils developed over an impermeable pan of hardened sand, later colonised by manuka. Be vigilant following the orange marker posts as a complex lattice of tracks has been bulldozed over the headland. The tracks are wide and firm.

The final 10 minutes over Scott Point to Kahokawa Beach, at the northernmost tip of Ninety Mile Beach, drops via wooden steps. From the southern side of the point there are postcard views of Ninety Mile Beach. The white tufts of rolling surf are shadowed by a gauze of spray, which thickens towards the distant horizon.

To Maori Ninety Mile Beach is known as Te Oneroa-a-Tohe, meaning 'the long beach of Tohe'. It is certainly a daunting prospect looking down the endless sands. The beach is approximately 55 miles (88 km) long. The source of the inaccurate English name is as hazy as the horizon. One theory is linked to an early European settler who grazed sheep near Ahipara at the southern end of the beach. In autumn he would drive them north up the length of the beach to Scott Point to graze. As the only Pakeha with reason to make the journey, he was often asked its length. His response of 'About ninety miles' became commonly used and the misnomer stuck.

It takes around 1 hour to walk along firm sand to reach Te Paki

Stream (Kauaeparaoa Stream), from where it is a further 1 hour to the carpark. The final leg involves walking along the bed of the shallow, sandy stream. If your boots are not waterproof, then wet feet are inevitable.

The vast surrounding dunes rise to over 150 m. Striking patterns etched by the wind are broken only by the tracks of toboggans. Dune riding is now common amongst those visiting Te Paki Stream by coach, but the tracks will soon be resculpted by the wind. The dune systems around Cape Maria Van Diemen and Te Paki Stream are the final product of sand accretion. Sediment transported by rivers from the central North Island volcanoes has been blown up the coast by the prevailing south-westerly winds and accumulated to form dunes.

Beware of vehicles on Ninety Mile Beach and at Te Paki Stream, which is the main northern access point for vehicles using the beach.

3

Cape Brett

Cape Brett protrudes 10 km into the Pacific, separating the open ocean from the labyrinth of waterways of the Bay of Islands. The walk takes you out to an isolated and raw coastline which offers panoramic views.

Grade	Hard
Time	6¹/₂ hours one-way
Access	From Russell head for Rawhiti by following Russell Road and Kempthorne Road, which merges with Manawaora Road. Turn left at the junction with Rawhiti Road. The start of the track is signposted just after Rawhiti in Hauai Bay. Secure parking is available at the end of Rawhiti Road, 1 km from the start of the track at Hartwells, Kaimarama Bay.
Notes	Before your departure a track fee must be paid at the DoC office in Russell. Walkers wishing to complete the trip in a day should contact Russell or Paihia information centres for details of boat operators who can collect you from the cape. Otherwise you must stay at Cape Brett Hut, an old lighthouse keeper's house that has been converted to a

21-person hut. You must contact DoC at Russell, who will give out the combination upon receipt of payment.

Cape Brett Track is wide and marked with orange triangles. The uneven track is occasionally muddy and always on a gradient. The first ascent from the walk's starting point leads to Oke Bay, a stunning beach sheltered from the wind. Scintillating golden sand sculptured into ripple patterns melts into the crystal waters lapping its edges. Steep cliffs smothered in pohutukawa rise behind and provide shade. A swim here on the return trip is just reward for the excursion.

The track climbs steadily and steeply to a picnic table (1 hour) at a viewpoint on the sheltered western side of the cape. Innumerable headlands, forest-capped islets and tranquil bays edge the clear turquoise waters. The reason for the naming of the Bay of Islands is startlingly evident from this elevated vantage point.

Over the next 45 minutes the track passes the junctions of tracks to Whangamumu and goes through a gate in an electric fence. Possum browsing is having a disastrous effect on the coastal vegetation, with pohutukawa especially vulnerable. It is hoped the fence, constructed in 1995 across the width of the peninsula, will reduce possum numbers – although entries in the hut book state that possums are still sometimes seen around the cape.

The next $2^1/_2$ hours involves the most strenuous walking, with frequent undulations along the ridge. Views are few and far between in the cool, shaded coastal forest. Watch for the signposted 45-minute detour to Deep Water Cove. This descends to sea level and is a refreshing spot for a swim on a hot day. Be careful of the shoreline rocks.

The main track exits the regenerating forest after 30 minutes and looks out towards the tip of Cape Brett. The thinning limb of the peninsula recedes to the vast ocean. On the southern seaward side the huge swells bombard the sheer cliffs in explosions of spray.

The last $1^1/_2$ hours of the track crosses grassland. In places it balances on a knife edge with sheer cliffs on either side. Be extremely careful in windy conditions: gusts can howl over the ridge from almost any direction. Stay low and pick a route carefully.

The hut is 10 minutes past the lighthouse near the foot of the hill. The Cape Brett lighthouse stands 150 m above sea level and was erected in 1909. A landing block and crane were used to unload the building materials, which must have been a treacherous operation in stormy conditions. The goods were then loaded onto a tramline powered by a whim. The route of the tramline is still evident today and is the easiest track to follow from the hut to explore the coast. The cast-iron sections of the lighthouse were formed in Price's foundry, in Thames, and bolted together on site. Cape Brett lighthouse is noteworthy because the lighting apparatus was the first in New Zealand to revolve in a mercury bath. This reduced the friction and thus the energy needed to keep the light revolving.

Three identical weatherboard houses were constructed for the lighthouse keepers and their families. They needed to be weather-tight and of solid construction to keep the ferocious elements at bay. Keepers ensured the light functioned properly, maintained the buildings, kept stock and communicated with passing vessels. The accommodation hut is an immaculately renovated house, with durable matai floorboards and a solid feel. Information boards on the wall bring to life the conditions the families faced and give a sense of the hardships involved.

In 1941 a military signal station was established on the site and, with the threat of a Japanese invasion in 1942, a radar station was built. The concrete footings of many structures remain and make interesting exploring.

4

Whangamumu Scenic Reserve

This stunning bay with well-preserved remnants of a former whaling station nestles at the foot of Cape Brett in the Bay of Islands. Sheltered from the open ocean and surrounded by forested headlands, the cove is a relaxing haven for boaties and walkers alike.

Grade	Easy
Time	2^1/$_2$ hours return
Access	From Russell head for Rawhiti by following Russell Road and Kempthorne Road, which merges with Manawaora Road. Turn left at the junction with Rawhiti Road. Look for the DoC sign at start of the track after 1 km. The adjoining property will provide secure parking for a small fee.

For 15 minutes the track squelches through sometimes muddy farmland and is marked with green-and-yellow posts. It then widens and becomes well formed, but is slippery in spots where the soil cover has been removed to expose clay. It soon reaches a lookout by the junction with the link to Cape Brett Track.

Entering Whangamumu Scenic Reserve, the track can again be slippery as it descends to the beach (20 minutes). Whangamumu Harbour is a deep, sheltered cove with a bronze-sand beach and shading pohutukawa. Sailing boats anchor in the sheltered waters while wavelets lap the serene shores. This is a delightful bay in which to pass the time.

Five minutes across the small promontory to the left is a whaling station that between the 1890s and 1940 intercepted humpback whales on their regular migration route to warmer waters. The whales were caught with buoyed nets anchored by a strong cable to nearby rocks, one now known as Net Rock, and were easily harpooned. Whangamumu was the only place in the world where whales were caught this way and the method was patented. After capture, the whales were towed to the harbour, cut up and boiled. Imagine the stench as they simmered for 36 hours in try-pots. The reek of bubbling blubber would have permeated the entire harbour. There is an eerie sense of death around the concrete foundations of the try-pots, which are still evident today.

In 1927, at the peak of the station's output, 74 whales were caught, yielding 388 tonnes of oil and 70 tonnes of bone dust. In 1940, following the sinking of the tanker *Niagara,* an oil slick changed the whales' migration path, forcing the closure of the station. Most of the men employed came from Rawhiti, and many of their descendants still live in the area. Whaling must have been in the blood of one local family, the Cooks, as some of the children were born at sea on whaling trips. The Cooks were notorious for using ambitious and dangerous fishing methods.

5

Island walks in
the Bay of Islands

The waters of the Bay of Islands are studded with islands ripe for exploration. A long human history has left a legacy that complements the location. Information centres in Russell and Paihia can advise on boat services to Urupukapuka, Motuarohia and Moturua Islands.

Urupukapuka Island

There are 66 archaeological sites on Urupukapuka Island, including eight pa. Terraces, ditches, storage pits and fortifications are all clearly distinguishable and many of them are explained by interpretive panels.

Grade	Medium
Time	4¹/₂ hours return
Access	Contact information centres in Russell or Paihia for advice on boat services to the island. Most boats will stop at Otehei Bay wharf. The start of the walk is signposted at the southern side of the bay.

The tracks on the island form two loops, both marked with green poles with a yellow band at the top. Climb the hill behind Otehei Bay to the signpost at the meeting point of the loops. There are two choices depending on how much time you have and how far you want to walk. To the right is a loop that takes $1^1/_2$ hours via Cable Bay. This shorter loop is grazed with sheep to minimise the fire risk. The more interesting track to the left explores the bulk of the island and takes approximately 3 hours. Both tracks follow the coastal fringe of the island along undulating, grassed tracks. There is little forest cover so views are generally expansive.

In 1772 Marc Joseph Marion du Fresne and his ill-fated French expedition noted many villages with palisades on Urupukapuka Island. These were probably inhabited by Ngare Raumati people, although the proximity to bountiful fishing grounds made the island desirable territory. In the early 1800s, despite skirmishes with Nga Puhi and Ngati Rehia, kainga (unfortified villages) still abounded on the island.

The main section of the walk weaves between open grassed areas and regenerating manuka forest. Occasionally the track drops to small, isolated beaches. At the northern part of the island the track follows the clifftop. Nearby islands seem close enough to touch, or swim to. The views are a microcosm of the Bay of Islands, with ancient pa sites perched on forested headlands, steep hillsides descending to sheltered beaches, and rocky islets protruding through the clear water.

Otiao Bay, on the north-western side of the island, is also named Indico Bay after Doro Indico, an Italian immigrant who married a New Zealander. They lived a subsistence lifestyle in a shanty beside the creek in the 1920s and 1930s, fishing and growing vegetables and, inevitably for an Italian, tomatoes.

Just south is a 30-minute detour to Oneura Bay (Paradise Bay). The track rejoins the main route over the hill back to Otehei Bay, where there is a café with toilets.

In 1926 American writer and passionate fisherman Zane Grey established a fishing camp at Otehei Bay. He erected tents and basic structures, and gained experience in catching the elusive marlin by venturing out with locals. The prize fish was rarely caught at that time and his stories were enough to attract a long list of wealthy clients, many from overseas. A more permanent fishing camp was built later.

Motuarohia Island

Motuarohia Island is actually two separate islands joined by a tombolo, or sandspit.

Grade	Easy
Time	20 minutes return
Access	Contact information centres in Russell or Paihia for advice on boat services to the island.

Follow the even track that climbs to a lookout platform. DoC staff with the enviable task of working in such a magnificent location have enhanced the final section with elaborate wooden steps. The views from the summit stretch in all directions and show the splendour of the Bay of Islands.

Motuarohia has an interesting architecture. On the southern side a beach stretches the length of the sandspit. On the northern side three shallow lagoons enclosed by rocky islets have scalloped the coastline so deeply the beaches back straight onto the southern beach. The rocky bottoms of the lagoons harbour abundant marine life and are ideal for snorkelling. DoC has constructed an interpretive snorkel trail with underwater plaques.

Motuarohia is also named Roberton Island after John Roberton, who lived here for a short time from 1839. He purchased the island from chiefs Warerahi, Meko and Rewa, and set about building a farmhouse and establishing a farm. Roberton drowned in 1840 (a fate coincidentally shared by his five brothers), but his widow stayed on the island. With her servant, Thomas Bull, she brought up her three children and Maketu, the wayward son of a Kororareka chief. Maketu felt his noble lineage permitted a carefree attitude and he resented being rebuked. After one instance of misbehaviour, he killed all five island residents. He was taken to Auckland and hanged, reputedly the first recipient of capital punishment in the colony.

On 29 November 1769 Captain Cook and his men landed on Motuarohia. His diary entry notes the island as well populated and substantially cultivated. His welcome was far from cordial and on being surrounded by a large party of threatening Maori, he ordered a shot to be fired at the young chief leading the party, causing a retreat.

The present landowner of Motuarohia has planted over 200,000 trees in an attempt to recreate the long-destroyed native forest. In 1978 a pair of kiwi was reintroduced to the predator-free island and the population has swelled to 17.

Moturua Island

This scenic reserve of regenerating bush has seen a great deal of suffering.

Grade	Easy
Time	2¹/₂ hours return
Access	Contact information centres in Russell or Paihia for advice on boat services to the island.

The track around the island is well formed and passes through long grass and forest, looping between beaches. It is only occasionally marked with green posts, but the route is followed easily enough. Most boats will land at Waipao Bay.

From 11 May 1772 Frenchman Marion de Fresne and his sailors camped on Moturua. Du Fresne had not found fresh produce on his journey to keep scurvy at bay among his crew. In desperate need of supplies and fresh water, and with very fatigued sailors, he quickly made Waipao Bay a hospital camp. His two vessels *Mascarin* and *Marquis de Castries* were in dire need of repairs, so a forge was constructed behind the beach. Sailors made reconnaissance trips for new masts and felled kauri spars in Clendon Cove under the command of M. Crozet.

The crew were very diligent in their observations of life in Maori villages and made detailed notes of the customs they witnessed. They were generally received warmly and offered hospitality. There was a constant exchange of gifts, including shellfish and fish. The French renamed Moturua Island as Marion Island.

Civil relations deteriorated when the French discovered that clothing and a musket had been stolen from the camp. Wariness of the Maori, who vastly outnumbered the sick crew, increased. While on a fishing trip to Orokawa Bay on the mainland, Marion du Fresne and his accompanying small crew were killed by a group of Maori. The exact reason is uncertain, although it has been suggested fishing in tapu waters and cutting firewood on burial sites contributed to the conflict between Maori and 'Marion's Tribe'. The hospital camp on Moturua was evacuated in anticipation of further attacks. The French became jittery and, under the assumed command of M. Crozet, 26 crew armed with muskets forced the evacuation of a pa. The French destroyed many abandoned villages, where they found the blood-stained clothes of their fellow seamen and evidence of cannibal feasts.

On 12 July 1772, nearly three years after Captain Cook had claimed New Zealand for Great Britain, New Zealand (known as 'Austral France' to the French) was formally claimed and the officers of the two ships buried a bottle at Waipao Bay. This artefact has never been found. It took M. Crozet and his beleaguered crew 10 months to limp back to France.

The walk around the island is divided into four sections, each traversing low hills between beaches and taking 20–30 minutes. From the eastern end of Waipao Bay climb the low hill to Otupono Bay. On the way to Waiwhapuku Bay look for kumara storage pits on the trackside. During World War II the control base for the mines laid in the Bay of Islands area was located here.

The track to Mangahawea Bay can be muddy and slippery, but the shorter section back to Waipao Bay is firmer. Another 15-minute return walk from the eastern end of the beach leads to Pupuha Pa, where remains of the housing and camp buildings from the World War II base can still be seen.

6

Whangaruru North Head walks

Perched on a rocky promontory south-east of Russell, Whangaruru North Head offers spectacular geology, and ocean and harbour views. The two walks can be combined to form a 2^{1}/$_{2}$–hour loop.

Ocean Beach

The open coast of Whangaruru North Head is exposed to the sea and rises spectacularly in a series of ridges dissected by swampy narrow valleys. At the outfall of each stream is a small sandy beach.

Grade	Medium
Time	1^{3}/$_{4}$ hours return
Access	From Ngaiotonga turn into Whangaruru North Road. Pass through the gate after 11 km and descend the hill to the campground at Puriri Bay, where there is parking. The toilets are open only during the summer. The track starts south of the campground from the top of the hill.

The signposted track is marked with occasional orange triangles. Follow the access road along the sometimes muddy grass track (15 minutes). The track now enters forest, and after 15 minutes reaches a signpost with options to head left to Bland Bay Lookout or right to Ocean Beach.

Heading right, the track hugs the clifftop through low manuka (30 minutes) then descends to spectacular Ocean Beach. This raw beach is surrounded on all sides by high, steep cliffs. The greywacke mudstone of Whangaruru North Head has been eroded to mesmerising rock formations that rise to nearly 200 m. A massive sea cave to the south sends up aquatic fireworks when an easterly swell is compressed within it. Mist from the spray-charged air rises up the cliffs, fuelled by the wind. This is an ocean spectacle to take time and admire.

Head inland for 15 minutes to the signposted detour to the trig (5 minutes return). Views look north over the sheltered and enclosed Whangaruru Harbour and reach past Helena Bay south to Mimi-whangata. Drop down the hill to Admirals Bay and the ranger's house (10 minutes). The farm track to the top of the hill south of Puriri Bay takes a further 15 minutes. The farmed area is the legacy of past grazing but other areas of the reserve have reverted to forest. Manuka and kanuka are abundant, and despite human modification, over 350 species of flora have been recorded on the varied terrain within the reserve.

Whangaruru means 'sheltered harbour' and the area was inhabited by hapu of Nga Puhi. At the end of the 1800s nearly 2000 Maori lived in the area. Many later worked in the gumfields, collecting kauri gum washed into the low-lying swamps.

Bland Bay Lookout

From Bland Bay Lookout it is evident that Whangaruru North Head is joined to the mainland by a tombolo, or sandspit, that has enclosed one side of Whangaruru Harbour.

Grade	Medium
Time	1^1/$_2$ hours return
Access	As for Ocean Beach walk

The route is marked with occasional orange triangles. For 15 minutes it climbs through muddy paddocks and then it enters the forest (15 minutes). Bear left at the signposted junction (the option to the right leads to Ocean Beach along the Ocean Beach Loop Track) and follow the ridge (20 minutes) to the signpost to the lookout (1 minute return).

A further 10 minutes along the main track there is a grass clearing with another lookout to Bland Bay. A contrast to the dramatic views of the Ocean Beach Walk, the more subdued vista takes in the collection of baches at Bland Bay. This was the main settlement of Whangaruru and was named in the late 1800s. Two pa flank the low, sandy neck, with Tewhau Pa sited on the northern side of Whangaruru Head.

The track drops for 20 minutes to a wetland (10 minutes) and reaches the road 200 m before the gate at the park entrance. It takes approximately 10 minutes to walk back to Puriri Bay along the road.

Northland

The thin finger of land north of the Auckland isthmus is dominated by the Kaipara Harbour to the west, while the predominantly rocky east coast is studded with innumerable bays, inlets and coves.

Hidden backwaters such as Mimiwhangata Coastal Park and Whananaki offer an intimacy that contrasts with the massive scale of the tracks around Bream Head near Whangarei.

7

Mimiwhangata Coastal Park

Mimiwhangata Coastal Park, midway between Russell and Whangarei, occupies a curved peninsula that ends in a high headland. The landscape is varied, with forested hills, low ridges, pastures, wetlands and wide beaches. On the western side, Mimiwhangata Bay is sheltered and offers a rejuvenating swim after a walk.

Grade	Easy/Medium
Time	Up to a full day, but itineraries can be devised to suit your preferred length of walk.
Access	Turn off Old Russell Road at Helena Bay and continue 7 km along unsealed Mimiwhangata Road. Mimiwhangata is signposted. There are toilets at the roadend.

Exploring Mimiwhangata Coastal Park requires a good sense of direction. There are no walking tracks, but a network of farm tracks allows visitors to reach its headlands, forest remnants, beaches, sand dunes and swamps. The best way to devise an itinerary is to find a high point, gain your bearings and set off in any direction that attracts your interest.

Threatened shorebirds, including New Zealand dotterels and variable oystercatchers, nest in shallow scrapes in the sand of the beaches and dunes. Around the greywacke cliffs mature pohutukawa and kowhai trees add splashes of colour in spring and summer. In the wetlands rare brown teal, spotless crakes and bitterns may make their presence felt, but the calls of brown kiwi and morepork can be heard only at night. In the protected waters of the marine park flourishes a wide range of sea life, include subtropical reef fish.

This peaceful place was once a bustling centre for Ngati Manaia. Pa dotted the hills, and in pre-European times the population may have been as high as 2000. Henry Charles Holman bought Mimiwhangata in 1840 from chief Puanaki. There followed a series of owners before New Zealand Breweries took over the land in 1962 with the intention of building a huge tourist resort. Locals and environmentalists made vigorous protests, establishing the Mimiwhangata Farm Park Trust in 1975. Thanks to their hard work visitors can now freely explore the hills, beaches and forests of Mimiwhangata Coastal Park.

8

Whananaki
Coastal Walkway

The Whananaki coast north-east of Whangarei is a repeating pattern of grassed spurs and gullies. The headlands dwindle to rocky points and pohutukawa and kauri mix with occasional puriri and kohekohe.

Grade	Medium
Time	2^1/$_4$ hours one-way 3^1/$_2$ hours one-way including detours
Access	There is no parking near the start of the track on McAuslin Road, so park at Sandy Bay Recreation Reserve at the northern end of Sandy Bay, where there are also toilets. It's approximately 1 km to the start of the track, signposted from the farm gate. In Whananaki South the walk is signposted by the footbridge at the end of Whananaki South Road. There is limited parking.
Notes	The Whananaki South end of the walk is tidal, so check tide times before departing. It is possible to return via the same route only if starting from the Sandy Bay end. Otherwise transport must be arranged.

The metalled farm track is marked with orange posts and undulates between sandy coves. The only two permitted access ways to beaches are signposted at the start of the walk and after 30 minutes.

For the first hour there is a snug feeling to this section of coastline. The high viewpoint allows full appreciation of the small-scale intimate coastal features. Shortly after the track becomes grassed there is a signposted detour to the *Capitaine Bougainville* monument (45 minutes return), a granite column at the end of the headland. The track has been worn through the long grass and weaves through plantations of youthful pines. When mature the monotonous exotic forest will provide stark contrast to the regenerating forest remnants in the gullies. The *Capitaine Bougainville* was a French freighter wrecked off the Whananaki coast in 1973. Sixteen lives were lost when a lifeboat capsized.

Return by the same track and continue north along a grassed farm track (45 minutes). This heads inland and the sounds of the ocean recede. The features change as the route follows a sandy 4WD track behind Whananaki Recreation Reserve, the consolidated low dunes and the beach. The sandy track to the left should be taken if there is doubt about the tide at Whananaki, which is a further 20 minutes.

A 400-m footbridge over the sand-choked Whananaki Inlet connects the two parts of the settlement. It is a charming and lackadaisical place where an atmosphere of decades gone by infuses the salt-laden breeze blowing in from the ocean beaches nearby.

Bear left behind the old-style baches. Walking the final 50 m over firm mudflats is not possible 1 hour either side of high tide without getting wet feet. If asked, the property owners on the estuary usually permit walkers to cross the front of their sections. This exercise is accompanied by a chat and fond farewells. If tide conditions do not allow a crossing of the soft mud, the only other route is to bear left along the sandy track opposite Whananaki Recreation Reserve, which exits near the roadend of Whananaki South Road.

9

Bream Head

The conspicuous jagged pinnacles of Bream Head, south-east of Whangarei, are the eroded remnants of a long-extinct volcano. Their superlative height grants spectacular views in all directions. The walk described here starts at Urquharts Bay and covers a route including Smugglers Bay and Peach Cove.

Grade	Hard
Time	5 hours one-way $6^1/_4$ hours one-way including side trip to Peach Cove $7^1/_2$ hours one-way including side trips to Smugglers Bay and Peach Cove
Access	The western end of the track is by the carpark at the end of Urquharts Bay Road. To start the Bream Head Track, head left for 10 minutes over farmland towards the base of Mount Lion and look for the signpost at the edge of the native forest. Otherwise walk straight across the farmland towards Smugglers Bay. The eastern end of the track is at Ocean Beach at the end of Ocean Beach Road. Turn right into Ranui Road just before the roadend and continue to the parking area with

	toilets. Walk south along Ocean Beach to the dunes and the start of the track.
Note	You must arrange transport at both ends as this walk is realistically achieved only in one direction.

Initially the track crosses poorly drained farmland along Woolshed Bay and is lined with orange posts (30 minutes). It heads for the remains of a World War II gun emplacement constructed secretly in 1942. Mounting a 6-inch naval gun without drawing attention must have been a trying exercise for the army, especially as the complex was on the western (townward) side of the head to shield it from enemy observation. The gun was fired only three times and never at an enemy vessel. The buildings of the remote-control room and generating shed were designed to look like farm buildings and are still reasonably intact. Above the window in the remote-control room is a hand-painted frieze of the landscape, with bearings marked beneath. The main point of difference with today's view is the absence of Marsden Point oil refinery. It constitutes a historical record of the landscape before scarring by human intervention.

Cross long grass for 20 minutes along a track marked with orange triangles. At the junction to Busby Head bear left over farmland and follow the orange posts to return to the carpark (30 minutes), or head right to continue to Ocean Beach.

The track to the pa at Busby Head is narrow but well formed. Hangi pits are now small depressions overgrown with vegetation, but a little searching reveals the larger storage pits. Kumara could be preserved for long periods in cool darkness, to be cooked when harvests were poor. Terraces were excavated on the steeper slopes to provide a flat base for dwellings and communal whare. After 10 minutes the track passes a signpost on the left to Smugglers Bay. This short section includes very slippery sections over exposed rocks. The detour to reach the tip of the headland and return to Smugglers Bay takes 30 minutes. It has limited views through the regenerating forest.

Smugglers Bay got its name in pioneer days when whisky used to be concealed in the dunes behind the bay to avoid customs duty at the port of Whangarei. Smugglers would unload the liquor then sail into port, returning to the bay at a later date to retrieve the booty. Three high middens rise from the rear of the bay and were most likely deposited by Ngati Wai and their ancestors Ngati Manaia. Archaeologists have sifted through the heaps and established the area was occupied for many centuries. Examination of the shells and bones has revealed a diet composed largely of fish and seafood.

Head up the hill towards the fenceline at the base of Mount Lion. The track is marked with orange triangles and is well formed but uneven. The toughest section of the walk now begins. Be prepared for a steep 1-hour climb to the summit of Mount Lion. Clearings in the vegetation are few and far between, reserving the best views for later in the walk.

For the next $1^1/2$ hours the track is shaded in a forest of puriri, kohekohe, kawakawa and other coastal species. Occasional tantalising views are glimpsed through the greenery. The track slowly descends the ridge to a signposted junction with Peach Cove Track, passing through a grazed area demarcated with an electric fence. It seems strange to see cattle grazing in the forest, but farmland overlaps with the DoC-administered reserve of Bream Head.

The track to Peach Cove Hut drops steeply (20 minutes). The hut can be booked at DoC in Whangarei and is 5 minutes inland from Peach Cove. A toilet is situated nearby. A small pebble beach breaks the otherwise rocky coastline at the foot of steep, forested cliffs overshadowed by the towering saw-tooth pinnacles of Bream Head.

Back on the main track the climb to the lookout at the summit of Bream Head takes approximately $1^1/4$ hours. The climactic ascent of the pinnacles involves a short, near-vertical rock face. Take extreme care and do not climb the pinnacle if unsure. This is not the place to get injured. If you are part of a large party, then take turns on the summit area as it is very small. Beware of strong wind gusts.

The views are distant and panoramic. Mount Moehau on the Coromandel Peninsula is clearly visible over 100 km away. Mount Hobson on Great Barrier Island looms over the ocean and Cape Rodney, the Hen and Chickens Group and Whangarei Harbour are all minuscule. This is a memorable vantage point.

You are standing atop a volcanic plug. Around 20 million years ago, volcanic activity formed cones, whose vents were filled with slowly cooling lava. These rocks have resisted the agents of weathering more than the layers of ash, pumice, lava and mud forming the surrounding cone. The peaks are the skeletal remains of the volcano's anatomy. As it rose, the andesite lava occasionally broke away from the main vent and formed splinter dykes such as Taurikura, at the eastern end.

To reach Ocean Beach retrace the final few steps from the summit and follow the ridge past the radar station (30 minutes). The final 45 minutes to the beach crosses open grassland and is marked with orange posts.

Greater Auckland

The Greater Auckland region has a diverse coastline that most strikingly shows off the characters of the west and east coasts. Both provide unique and inspiring atmospheres. On the west coast the spiritually uplifting and awe-inspiring black sands can be explored around Piha. The intimate, serene and cosy east coast beaches of the Waitemata Harbour and Hauraki Gulf counterpoint those on the west coast; tiny indentations in the sandstone cliffs and the shelter of the gulf islands provide ideal walking locations.

The islands of the Hauraki Gulf have their own unique histories and characteristics. From the remains of Auckland's coastal war defences on Waiheke Island to the recreated avian paradise of Tiritiri Matangi, Greater Auckland's coast makes for many a rewarding excursion.

10

Tawharanui Regional Park

Tawharanui Regional Park sits on the tip of a limb of resistant grey-wacke, the most extensive finger of land reaching into the northern Hauraki Gulf. Compared with the relative intimacy of the Waitemata Harbour's inlets and coves, the Tawharanui Peninsula has views on a grander scale: the Moehau Range of the Coromandel Peninsula, Great Barrier Island, Little Barrier Island, the Hen and Chickens Group and Bream Head.

From 1877, when the peninsula fell into European hands, the land was cleared of kauri and converted to pasture. Successive families farmed the headland until the Auckland Regional Authority bought it in 1973. Tracks crisscross the park, most on a metalled surface or over pasture. There are three loop walks through pasture and forest, over craggy coastal rocks and along golden-sand beaches.

Tawharanui Regional Park is signposted along Tokatu Road from past Matakana. It is administered by Auckland Regional Council. Picnic tables and parking are at the lagoon carpark on the entrance road, and Anchor Bay at the roadend. There are toilets by the information buildings and at Anchor Bay.

It will take a full day to explore the entire park. Take some time to familiarise yourself with the track layout on the information panels, as this will aid later navigation.

South coast loop

This walk takes in a lagoon, rocky coastline and regenerating forest.

Grade	Easy
Time	$2^1/4$ hours return
Access	The start of the track is signposted from the lagoon carpark.

The Jones Bay lagoon is a mix of fresh water from local streams and salt water from tidal influx. The lagoon outlet houses green-lipped mussels and pipi, while eel grass forms carpets around the edges. It was formed in the early nineteenth century when the area was quarried for gravel.

Three hours either side of low tide it is possible to follow the coastline from Jones Bay to Maori Bay on the Maori Bay Coast Walk (1 hour). Pick your way carefully over coastal boulders, rock shelves and pebble-strewn beaches. The crevices of rock pools are home to rock snails, pulmonate snails and fragile limpets, while crabs scurry across the sandy bottoms of the pools. There are views of Kawau Island's northern side, which shelters the sinuous coastline around the eastern arm of Mahurangi Harbour.

After approximately 45 minutes keep an eye out for a large rock that resembles an unfurling palm frond. Maori Bay and the South Coast Track are just the other side of the next headland. Be vigilant, as the steep grass track inland is easy to miss.

The final $1^1/4$ hours on the South Coast Track complements the coastal section and passes through regenerating forest and pasture. The walk is signposted and marked with white-banded posts. The park was once smothered in towering kauri, which were logged and used for house and boat building. Vigorous regeneration reclothed the hills with manuka but this was stripped for use as firewood before the conversion to the pasture seen today. The remaining coastal forest is composed of puriri, pohutukawa and tawa. The dense understorey of red mapou, kawakawa and karaka forms a shady corridor on the return to the carpark.

Tokatu Point

Tokatu Point is the tip of Tawharanui Peninsula and commands extensive views of the Hauraki Gulf.

Grade	Medium
Time	3¹/₂ hours return
Access	The start of the track is signposted from Anchor Bay carpark.

Head east from the carpark, follow the metalled coast road and cross the footbridge (10 minutes). The start of the North Coast Track is signposted and undulates over farmland for 45 minutes past a trig to the junction with Tokatu Point Lookout Track. From the trig the views stretch over the outer Hauraki Gulf with memorable sea and sky scapes. Cape Rodney closes off the coastal vistas past Omaha Bay to the north.

It will take around 1¹/₂ hours to explore the headland via Tokatu Loop Track or just 30 minutes to walk directly to the lookout at Tokatu Point. Here there are views of the outer Hauraki Gulf islands punctuating the horizon. The harsh conditions experienced on the exposed point have curious effects on the vegetation. Rare prostrate manuka forms low clumps: the familiar tree cannot tolerate the wind, so reacts by growing low to the ground like a shrub.

The geological history of the Tawharanui Peninsula is best illustrated at Tokatu Point. The underlying greywacke rocks have been folded, then uplifted and overlain by sedimentary sand and siltstone deposits. Later weathering by wave and wind and dissection by stream runoff has sculpted the craggy cliffs and rock stacks seen today.

An alternative return route via the partially metalled Fisherman's Track is marked with red-banded posts. This cuts through coastal forest remnants, characterised by rimu and kauri on the ridge tops, with tawa, taraire and puriri lining the gullies and valleys. The puriri trees leave a carpet of pink flowers on the forest floor. Another return route is along the Ecology Trail, marked with yellow-banded posts, which provides the best walking surface. All return routes lead to Anchor Bay and take approximately 1¹/₄ hours.

Westend Track

The scalloped beaches of the northern coast are tempting places to waste time. A sprinkling of shells decorates the firm, fine, golden sand, and dune fields recede behind.

Grade	Easy
Time	1¹/₂ hours return
Access	The start of the track is signposted from Anchor Bay carpark.

The track follows a low ridge over pasture (15 minutes) before bearing left through a cattleyard along a metalled farm track. Tawharanui Regional Park, like some other parks administered by Auckland Regional Council, is a working farm. As well as providing revenue, these 'model' farms are superb examples of how farming, conservation and recreation can coexist in areas with huge land pressures.

The undulating climb over sometimes muddy pasture to Pohutukawa Lookout takes 30 minutes. Little Barrier Island is the dominant feature of the horizon. The track then drops to the beach (15 minutes).

A shortcut signposted from just after the cattleyard cuts 15 minutes and the gradient out of the walk to the western end of Anchor Bay.

Follow the beach around Comets Rocks and Flat Rock to return to Anchor Bay (30 minutes). A pa site at the western end of Anchor Bay shows evidence of a defensive ditch, three food pits, a lookout platform and levelled terraces. Tawharanui was thought to have been inhabited by hapu of the Te Kawerau people and archaeological surveys of middens have revealed a diet rich in marine food sources.

11

Long Bay Regional Park

This walk, beginning in the most northerly of Auckland's East Coast Bays, offers a mix of lush coastal forest and rocky shore habitats protected by a marine reserve. The Vaughan Homestead and park facilities make any visit memorable.

Grade	Medium
Time	2³/₄ hours return
Access	From East Coast Road turn into Glenvar Road and continue through the settlement of Long Bay to Beach Road. The park entrance is on the left. The road leads past picnic areas, toilets and children's playgrounds. The start of the track is signposted at the roadend, before the Vaughan Homestead.

After a 5-minute detour to a World War II gun emplacement, the route follows a metalled track through coastal forest of puriri, taraire and mature pohutukawa. As you enter the farmland look for white-banded marker posts next to the grass track, which may be muddy after rain. The track undulates with steps constructed on the hills (1 hour).

At Piripiri Point the track bears left and arrives at the Okura River mouth (15 minutes). Three hours either side of low tide it is possible to return to Pohutukawa Bay following the base of the cliffs (45 minutes).

The coastline of the track forms part of the Long Bay–Okura Marine Reserve, established in 1995 to protect all marine life. The rock platform and subtidal reefs are rich marine habitats. As the waters head to the sea they become progressively less sheltered and this exposure is reflected in the life that abounds there.

Below the mean tide mark the rocky reefs are gnawed by waves, and forests of large brown seaweeds writhe in the currents like eels. Oysters and barnacles smother the edges of the rock shelf, while chitons shelter in rock hollows. Showers of Neptune's necklace adorn the stepped surface. Cat's eyes, periwinkles and whelks also encrust the rocks. Occasional crevices expose golf-ball sponges and kina.

The rock shelf can be slippery where there is an algal film. Try and pick a route over the barnacle zone (above the oysters) as they provide grip and are a safe distance away from the cliffs. The sandstone and mudstone layers of the Waitemata series form an impressive backdrop. The rock was formed through the deposition of mud and sand in a deep marine basin around 20 million years ago. Compaction and subsequent uplift have exposed the layers to their present height, although they are now being reclaimed by the sea. The rock shelf you are walking on has formed over the last 6500 years, since the stabilisation of sea levels. Erosion by wave action has chiselled the rock shelf from the former cliff face at its margin.

At Pohutukawa Bay pohutukawa branches provide shade for a moment's relaxation. It is an ideal spot for a summer picnic if you are comfortable among the nude bathers.

After a 30-minute walk back to the carpark, take time to examine the Vaughan Homestead. It was constructed from local kauri and puriri by George Vaughan in 1863. The previous year he purchased 600 ha of land and his descendants farmed the area for a century. The building was added to over its lifetime and lovingly restored to its present condition between 1993 and 1995 by the Torbay Historical Society.

12

Piha walks

The black-sand beach of the west coast's Piha is a place of uplifting grandeur, guaranteed to nourish the soul and revitalise the spirit. Walks from both ends of the beach explore some of its hidden treats.

Lion Rock

Lion Rock stands like a sentry at the mouth of Piha Stream. Its iconic profile is symbolic of Piha.

Grade	Easy/Medium
Time	30 minutes return
Access	Lion Rock is the prominent landmark at the mouth of the Piha Stream. There is ample parking on the beachfront on Seaview Road.

To Te Kawerau-a-Maki Lion Rock was an obvious site for a defensive pa. The flatter summit was a tihi, the last place of refuge in an attack. The rock itself was known as Te Piha, in recognition of the wave patterns on its seaward side, which resemble those at the prow of a waka.

It is a shock to find the initial few steps uneven. After negotiating the treacherous beginnings, the track becomes stepped with rails and benches to pause on. The top section is closed.

Lion Rock is a magnificent example of an offshore stack, a sister feature to Nun Rock at the southern end of the beach. The more resistant cap of rock has protected its base, while weaker rocks in the vicinity have been broken down by the unceasing actions of wave and wind.

Whites Beach

Artists specialising in environmental sculptures use Whites Beach as a preferred location. These temporary exhibits are eventually reclaimed by the elements.

Grade	Medium
Time	1¹/₂ hours return
Access	Park in the carpark at the end of North Piha Road and walk along the beach past the caves. The start of Laird Thomson Track is signposted on the right from the northern end of North Piha Beach.

Whites Beach is reached by following Laird Thomson Track and Rose Track over the northern headland. Laird Thompson Track is well maintained and climbs for 15 minutes to a junction. The track on the left leads to a lookout (5 minutes return). Behind the waltzing flax leaves the entire expanse of Piha recedes to Nun Rock at the southern end, and Lion Rock stands proudly above beachgoers scurrying like ants. Head right for 10 minutes to where Rose Track is signposted on the left. It's a further 15 minutes down to Whites Beach.

Whites Beach was named after John White, an early ethnographer with a keen interest in Maori culture. In the days when little was known by Europeans about Maori customs and protocol, his research helped educate early settlers. He negotiated the initial purchase of coastal land from Maori.

The beach is often less crowded than Piha, probably because of its inaccessibility. You have to work a little to get here but the rewards are worth the effort. High cliffs smothered in flax, manuka and pohutukawa rise steeply around the beach. Westerly winds skim salt spray from the wave caps and billow it steadily up the hillside. Don't leave until you have explored the deep sea cave at the northern end of the beach.

Tasman Lookout

From Tasman Lookout Track there are magnificent views of Piha, The Gap, Taitomo Island and Nun Rock.

Grade	Easy/Medium
Time	30 minutes return
Access	The start of the track is signposted from the southern end of Piha. There is parking nearby.

Tasman Lookout Track is a well-maintained track at the southern end of Piha. After an initial climb there is a lookout with views north over the beach. The bench above The Gap is an obligatory stop. It offers a view over the break in the rocks between Taitomo Island and the rock shelf on the mainland. When there is a big swell, which occurs with relative frequency on this section of Auckland's west coast, water is forced through the break and explodes in orgies of froth and foam. It is an awesome spectacle, making it easy to lose a lot of time here. On the far side of Taitomo Island is Nun Rock. The exposure to the elements has streamlined its seaward face.

Right: The soft sands of Spirits Bay, near Cape Reinga, leave a temporary reminder of your passage until the approaching tide remoulds the beach.

Below: The massive dunes around Te Paki Stream rise to over 150 m and form the most substantial dune systems in the country.

Left: The impressive tip of Cape Brett recedes in a knife-edged cliff to the lighthouse.

Below: Urupukapuka Island, viewed here from Cape Brett Track, is one of the sumptuous islands studding the turquoise waters of the Bay of Islands.

Right: A gauze of sea spray rides up the cliffs and headlands of Whangaruru North Head.

Above: The arching peninsula at Mimiwhangata shelters a calm bay from the open ocean.

Left: The granite monument to the 16 sailors who lost their lives on the Capitaine Bougainville *is a short detour from the Whananaki Coastal Walkway.*

Right: The jagged pinnacles of Bream Head are flanked with dense coastal forest and steep cliffs.

Left: The uplifted headland of greywacke at Tokatu Point is the culmination of a walk to the tip of Tawharanui Regional Park.

Right: Sunsets over west coast beaches such as Piha are always a memorable sight.

Below: The baches on Rangitoto are testimony to the island's status as a haven for Auckland residents.

Left: The remains of Auckland's coastal defences at Stony Batter invite exploration both above and below ground.

Below: Mesmerising views are characteristic of the Coromandel Walkway.

13

Tiritiri Matangi Island

Before the arrival of humans, the Hauraki Gulf island of Tiritiri Matangi supported a vibrant ecosystem dominated by avian residents flourishing in the absence of predators. The introduction by Maori of the kiore (rat) and dog had a devastating effect on the defenceless species, some of them flightless. Land clearance for cultivation and hunting of birds for food further reduced the populations. With the advent of European settlers most of the remaining forest was burned and opened up for farming.

Since the late 1970s community initiatives and government protection have seen Tiritiri Matangi replanted with nearly 300,000 native seedlings. Rare and endangered bird species have been reintroduced to the now predator-free island. Today Tiritiri Matangi offers an accessible and enlightening glimpse of what the Hauraki Gulf islands once were.

Grade	Easy/Medium
Time	Full day
Access	The start of the walk is signposted from the wharf.
Note	Auckland information centres can advise on times of Fullers ferry departures from the downtown ferry terminal and Gulf Harbour.

Although the tracks on Tiritiri Matangi are signposted, the network of tracks is extensive. It is a good idea to pick up a map at the ferry office. There are toilets at the lighthouse area, the wharf and Hobbs Beach.

This route describes a clockwise loop of the island from the wharf. It follows the Hobbs Beach, Kawerau, Ngati Paoa, North East Bay and Eastern Tracks to the lighthouse, then finishes with the Wattle Track returning to the wharf. The loop takes approximately 4 hours to walk, but will undoubtedly take longer with all the distractions.

The first Maori settlers were from Te Kawerau-a-Maki, who remain the tangata whenua. They named the island Tiritiri Matangi, which means 'tossed by the wind'. Many Europeans now shorten the name to simply Tiri.

Ngati Paoa started incursions but were defeated by Te Kawerau, who remained on the island until 1821, when Hongi Hika and Nga Puhi attacked in a series of devastating raids. When Te Kawerau trickled back in 1837, Europeans had already taken over the island.

Settlement of disputes in the Maori Land Court in 1867 gave title to the government. In 1894 Joseph Schollum obtained the lease and the right to farm the island, which was transferred to Francis Dennis in 1896. In 1901 Edward John Hobbs took on the lease and this family connection lasted until 1971 when title was granted to the Hauraki Gulf Maritime Park Board. The legacy of the Hobbs family is remembered in the naming of Hobbs Track.

Hobbs Track takes 15 minutes one-way and departs from the wharf. Head left (signposted Kawerau Track) along the narrow track as it skirts the coastline, passing nesting boxes of blue penguins and crossing pebble beaches on a few occasions. The blue penguin is the smallest penguin species in the world. The birds come to the shore around Hobbs Beach to roost in rock crevices, under tree roots or in artificial rock burrows constructed by volunteers. These have shuttered viewing windows allowing a glimpse of the nest activity.

It takes 10 minutes to Hobbs Beach and the junction with Hobbs Track on the right, but head left along the beach towards Kawerau Track. This takes 30 minutes one-way on a mostly metalled track. It traverses a boardwalk through shaded coastal forest, climbing gently. Veer left at the junction although right will eventually meet up with Kawerau Track again.

When the government's 100-year lease of Tiri expired in 1971, it was decided the island should be made into a sanctuary for endangered birds, involving the restoration of the forest and associated ecosystems. Ray and Barbara Walter, the former lighthouse keepers, were entrusted with the job of island keepers, a task they still carry out with passion, care and vitality today.

It was strikingly evident Tiri needed a helping hand to speed up its recovery. A nursery was set up in 1983 to propagate once-common native plants such as pohutukawa, coprosma, kohekohe, puriri, karaka and cabbage trees. A few years later taraire, five finger and pigeonwood seedlings were also planted. Since the nursery was initiated, nearly 300,000 seedlings of 38 species have been planted on the island, mainly by volunteers and school groups. This forest is best exhibited in the boardwalked section of Kawerau Track, constructed to help protect shallow-rooting trees and provide an easier walking surface.

At the exit from the forest, head left to the junction with Tiritiri Matangi Pa Track. This 5-minute detour discovers the old pa site. Back at the junction bear left over the grassy vehicle track, passing the junction with another branch of Kawerau Track, to Ngati Paoa Track.

The vehicle track takes 40 minutes one-way. Head left, passing the junction on the right, which is the completion of the loop of the Ngati Paoa Track. It's 15 minutes to a 5-minute detour to North East Point, then 15 minutes and a descent through a gully to the start of Eastern Track. The views along this section are more expansive with the low vegetation cover. A more rugged and remote feel begins to envelop.

Eastern Track is a mixture of grass, metal and exposed earth (1 hour one-way). It weaves along the north-east coast, passing various junctions with tracks heading inland. Pohutukawa Cove is the natural stopping point for a break. While many visitors to Tiri will concentrate their attention on the wharf and lighthouse area, this northern coast is less frequented and a peaceful place for lunch. The rocky coastline has been scalloped by the ferocious action of waves into a convoluted form, with numerous islets, reefs and collapsed rock stacks. Keep following the coastline until the track climbs towards the lighthouse.

In the lighthouse area is a gift shop and information office. Tiritiri Matangi's lighthouse was constructed from sections that were built in England and bolted together on site. It is 20 m high and the light is

91 m above sea level. Built at a cost of £5288, it first started shining on 1 January 1865 and was originally fuelled by a wick and whale oil. This was converted to acetylene gas in 1925 and then diesel-generated electricity in 1955. The installation of an 11 million-candlepower xenon lamp in 1956 – powered by a 5-km-long undersea cable from the mainland – made it one of the most powerful lights in the world at that time. Now solar panels and a battery bank power the light, which flashes once every 15 seconds and can be seen for 18 nautical miles (33 km).

From the lighthouse head down the metalled wharf road and veer left at the signposted junction with Wattle Track. This metalled track with boardwalks has frequent benches from which to observe the endemic birdlife in the low canopy.

This is the best place for spotting the prolific and tuneful avian residents of Tiri. With pest eradication programmes and the reintroduction of endangered species from other island sanctuaries, the bird population is now thriving. Interaction is possible with ground-dwelling birds such as inquisitive takahe, which roam free especially around the lighthouse. Kiwi forage through the forest floor litter at night and semi-flightless kokako scurry through the understorey disseminating their hauntingly melodic song.

Watch for the ubiquitous honeyeaters such as tui and bellbirds, which with the endangered stitchbird help to pollinate the nectar-producing shrubs and trees. Saddlebacks, robins and whiteheads dart around at eye level providing constant interest in the forest interior.

High above kaka screech and display their scarlet underwing markings. Harrier hawks glide on the updraughts and black-backed and red-billed gulls hover above the coastal margins. Over 75 bird species have been recorded on or close to Tiri, seven of which are endangered species unlikely to be encountered on the mainland. Tiritiri Matangi is a glimpse of the past. Although not fully replicating New Zealand's former natural glory, Tiri is as close as we get today. It is an open sanctuary ripe for enjoyment, discovery and inspiration, a living lesson on how community action and scientific intervention can recreate a paradise once lost.

14

Rangitoto Island

Rangitoto is the major natural landmark of the Auckland metropolitan area. Its unmistakable volcanic form provides a stunning backdrop to views in the Auckland region. It also serves as a reminder of the restless forces beneath the city.

The conical peak rises as high as 259 m and its primeval landscape of bare scoria rock, slowly being enveloped by hardy vegetation, provides the walker with a unique atmosphere. Relics of permanent settlement such as baches, shipwrecks and fortifications impart a human dimension to Rangitoto's fragile shores.

The beginnings of the island's Maori name are unclear. Some experts say Rangitoto means 'sky reaching', while earlier translations render it as 'red' or 'bloody sky'. This suggests early migrants from Polynesia may have seen it during one of its eruptions. Another theory suggests Rangitoto is a shortened form of Te Rangi-i-totonga-a-Tama-Te-Kapua, which means 'the days bleeding of Tama Te Kapua'. This notable captain of the Arawa waka is said to have done battle in Islington Bay.

Various myths have been conferred upon the island. One tells of Pupuke Moana, a mountain that rose from the site of present-day Lake Pupuke. The mountain was cast by a demi-god to its present site in a mighty show of strength.

Another traditional story refers to the family of giants named the Children of the Fire Gods. After a quarrel their father became angry and cursed the fire god Mahuika. She retaliated with a ferocious earthquake, turning the giants to stone and sinking them into the ground. This formed Lake Pupuke and meanwhile Rangitoto rose from the ground.

Early Maori use of Rangitoto was as a burial place, a lookout in times of war and a parrot reserve. However, the harshness of the environment, with little fresh water or cultivable soil, deterred settlement of the island, with nearby Motutapu proving more hospitable.

On 17 January 1854 Rangitoto was sold to the Crown for £15 by chief Ngatai of Ngati Paoa.

The summit via McKenzie Bay and Summit Road descriptions apply to a shorter clockwise loop, following McKenzie Bay Road, Summit Road and Summit Track. The longer loop walk returns from the summit along the eastern flank of the volcano via Islington Bay. The return to Rangitoto wharf is along the Coastal Track.

Summit loop via McKenzie Bay

This invigorating loop walk takes in regenerating forest, the sandy beach at McKenzie Bay and the 360-degree view from the summit of Rangitoto Island.

Grade	Medium
Time	3^1/$_2$ hours return 4 hours return including detour to lava caves
Access	From Rangitoto wharf, walk inland up Summit Walk for 5 minutes, past the information shelter. To take the signposted track on the left through the Kidney Fern Glen, continue past the signpost on the left to McKenzie Bay.
Note	Information centres in Auckland can advise on the times of Fullers ferry departures from the downtown ferry terminal.

In the Kidney Fern Glen luminescent green kidney ferns adorn the trackside, providing a unique and surreal atmosphere to the walk. The kidney fern is a filmy fern with a delicate kidney-shaped lobed frond. The intense green is best demonstrated after periods of rain. Here on Rangitoto the fern forms a dense community, carpeting the forest floor with its fragile tissue-like foliage.

After 10 minutes the track veers right towards McKenzie Bay on a wide metalled road, passing two junctions. The first leads through the Kowhai Grove, but continue along the main track to another junction on the left to Flax Point (15 minutes return). It's 50 minutes to the junction near McKenzie Bay (5 minutes return), where there are toilets. On this section the track dips then heads a little inland through pohutukawa forest and lava fields.

Rangitoto is notable for displaying all stages of forest development from colonisation of bare scoria to flourishing forest. Despite the apparent inhospitality of the landscape over 250 species of flowering plant and native trees and 40 species of fern inhabit the jagged crevices of the scoria surface. Numerous lichens, mosses and liverworts are the first agents of soil formation. They draw moisture from underground reservoirs of water filtered through the haphazard rocky surface. The dark surface of the scoria holds the sun's heat and provides the ideal habitat for humidity- and moisture-loving colonisers, whose embryonic soils provide sustenance for crevice plants such as *Peperomia* and *Psilotum nudum*. Once small communities of leaf-bearing plants are established, coastal forests similar to those on the mainland follow.

Rangitoto has some large pohutukawa forests, especially on the coastal rim. As the roots delve in the rock crevices to exploit the subsurface moisture, the growing trees shed leaf litter for soil formation and provide shade for koromiko, mingimingi and puka. Pohutukawa is thus a nursery species, engendering the formation of forest islands that eventually link to form fully fledged forests. Some unusual hybridisation has occurred on Rangitoto, the most notable between pohutukawa and tree rata, forming a variation in leaf characteristics.

After 50 minutes' climbing on the Summit Road, passing the junctions with Wilson Park Track and an access road, follow the boardwalk on the right. This takes 15 minutes to reach a signpost from where the summit is a further 5 minutes.

This loop descends the Summit Walk for 10 minutes to the 30-minute detour to the lava caves. Take care following the yellow-topped green marker posts over the lava field, as these lead to the lava caves, one of which can be walked through. Take a torch.

The first European to discover the caves was Mr W. Wilson in 1912. Lava caves are formed when the surface of liquefied lava cools while a molten river within the hardened outer shell drains away to leave a cavity. These curious geological features have an eerie quietness far removed from the fiery volcanic processes that created them. Where there is now emptiness there was once a river of fire flowing with the power of a juggernaut. The caves are a memorable diversion from the overground features.

After a further 10 minutes on the main track, passing the junction with Wilson Park Track, there is a boardwalk with interpretive panels on the geology of the island. The track takes 40 minutes to descend to the wharf and is wide and well formed through scoria fields.

The city of Auckland lies directly above a hot spot, a large pool of molten rock that periodically spawns a smaller bubble of magma. Through convection this rises towards the surface, eventually working its way through the crust to disgorge its contents as a volcano. Rangitoto is the most recent addition to the Auckland Volcanic Field. The earliest volcanoes erupted 100,000–140,000 years ago, but of Auckland's 48 volcanoes 32 have appeared in the last 30,000 years.

Rangitoto stands as the proud aristocrat of all Auckland's volcanoes. It is larger than all the others combined and the only one to have erupted through sea water. Around 600 years ago the initial rumblings were followed by an explosive outpouring of ash that buried a settlement on Motutapu. The magma that followed flowed easily, building up the attenuated curves that make Rangitoto so distinctive. The shape is known as a shield volcano.

Summit loop via McKenzie Bay and Islington Bay

This longer loop walk adds to the mix a visit to the shipwrecks of Boulder Bay and the baches of Islington Bay. Boulder Bay was also known as

Wrecks Bay and was once a popular beachcombing spot for Islington Bay residents. The wreckage of abandoned vessels washed ashore fuelled campfires and flotsam was often taken for use in the baches.

Grade	Medium/Hard
Time	5¹/₂ hours return from Rangitoto wharf 6¹/₂ hours return including detour to Boulder Bay
Access	From Rangitoto wharf walk past the information shelter and follow the signpost on the left to McKenzie Bay.
Note	Auckland information centres can advise on times of Fullers ferry departures from the downtown ferry terminal.

Make your way to the summit via McKenzie Bay as in the last walk. Then retrace the final 5 minutes from the summit along the board-walk to Summit Road and continue right. Head down the hill for 45 minutes to the junction on the left with Boulder Bay Track. This detour takes 1 hour return. For 10 minutes the track crosses open lava fields. The scoria pieces are unconsolidated and it is necessary to concentrate to keep your footing. On entering the forest the track narrows. It is occasionally marked with orange triangles and yellow-and-green posts.

During the Depression two retired coal hauling vessels were beached at Boulder Bay. A few rotting timbers with metal pins and rusting protrusions piercing the water are the only remains today.

Back on Summit Road it is 5 minutes to the junction with the Coastal Walk, which takes 2 hours one-way. Turn right and follow the coast of Islington Bay. The bay was originally named Oruawharu Bay. The name Drunken Bay was later conferred because, in the days of sail, crews would often rest there to sober up before the outward journey. It was renamed Islington Bay after Lord Islington, governor of New Zealand from 1910 to 1912.

Rangitoto had been set aside as a recreation reserve in 1890 by Devonport Borough Council. It soon became apparent a landing wharf for day trippers was necessary and work was completed in 1897. At the same time Pioneer Track to the summit was opened, providing incentive for more visitors.

By the 1920s Rangitoto was gaining popularity as a weekend sojourn and baches began to sprout along the coastline. In 1925 the use of convict labour was approved and construction commenced on a road to the summit. Work progressed following the western shoreline and then traversed the island to Islington Bay, providing access from Rangitoto wharf to the summit.

Rangitoto's baches were pieced together using discarded building materials and healthy doses of ingenuity. The resulting edifices were models of functionalism, and today they still exude nostalgic charm. By 1935 there were 52 baches strung along the foreshore at Islington Bay and two years later there were 121 buildings on the island.

Damning local-authority reports in the 1930s claimed the unique natural features of Rangitoto were threatened by the presence of the baches. Despite protests from the Rangitoto Island Protection League, composed of bach owners and island residents, a government decision in 1938 forbade any more building permits, prohibited the sale or transfer of existing premises and gave residents 20 years' notice to leave the island.

In 1956 the benefits of having the residents were acknowledged. The control of introduced pests, protection of the rare biota from thieves and their guardianship of the island was finally appreciated. Existing residents were granted residency on the island for the rest of their natural lives. In 1968 the Hauraki Gulf Maritime Park Board took control of Rangitoto. Guardianship has now passed to the Department of Conservation.

At Yankee wharf there is a 10-minute detour to the controlled-mine base. During World War II, neighbouring Motutapu Island became the scene of fervent activity. A fire command post was built on the summit of Rangitoto, from where some of Auckland's coastal defences were organised. At the controlled-mine base the navy rigged a chain of mines that could be detonated if the enemy approached Auckland harbour. A wharf near the base was constructed for the Americans who spearheaded the defensive operations and the legacy of this intervention remains in the naming of Yankee wharf.

From Yankee wharf the track follows a formed route over the lava fields for 30 minutes before entering forest for 1 hour. Watch for skinks scurrying between rock crevices. The coastal forest provides welcome shade in the searing summer heat of Rangitoto's bare scoria rock. The track undulates and can be very uneven. It finishes 5 minutes from Rangitoto wharf.

15

Stony Batter

This walk on Waiheke Island explores the tunnel system associated with Auckland's wartime coastal defences. Between the two world wars, military strategists realised an enemy cruiser could exploit deep water near Motutapu and Rakino and use the protection of the islands to fire shells over Rangitoto at the city and its wharves, railways, port and naval bases. The government decided to block off the Hauraki Gulf by constructing two sets of guns. The remains of the infrastructure give a graphic reminder of the wartime initiatives mounted to protect New Zealand's coastline.

Grade	Easy
Time	40 minutes return
Access	Hire a car or arrange taxi transport from the ferry wharf. In Onetangi turn into Waiheke Road and follow the signposts to Stony Batter. There is no public transport to Stony Batter.
Notes	Auckland information centres can advise on times of Fullers ferry departures from the downtown ferry terminal and Devonport. The tunnel complex is open every day except Christmas

Day. Hours are 9.30 am to 3.30 pm but longer in summer and holiday periods – check the three blackboards around the island for opening times (Matiatia on the left past the carpark, Onetangi by the Hall and the Stony Batter carpark). Tours take around 1 hour but vary according to interest and fitness levels. The cost is $5 per person or $20 per family. The suggested entry donation is $2 and powerful torches (a necessity) can be hired for $5. The museum/information room has pamphlets and maps for sale.

From the carpark follow the metalled access road for 20 minutes to the signposted tunnel entrance. Walking along the road it is easy to understand why the site was chosen for the linchpin defences of Auckland city. The views not only stretch south to the Firth of Thames and Hauraki Plains, but also extend in all directions from Cape Colville to Cape Rodney.

In this farmed area andesitic boulders interspersed with grazing sheep create a curious landscape. The boulders, which give rise to Stony Batter's name, were also used to make aggregate for the vast quantities of concrete needed to construct the huge complex of underground fortifications.

Above ground the remains of the World War II guns are strikingly evident and easily explored by wandering through the paddocks between the gun pits, ventilation shafts and derelict buildings. However, for the best appreciation of the immensity of the gun emplacement infrastructure, take a walk through the vast underground network. A torch is essential.

Had you been an Auckland resident during World War II, the problems of city living would not have revolved around traffic, pollution and crime. The greatest apparent threat to your security would have been an enemy ship sneaking into the Waitemata Harbour and lobbing shells over Motutapu.

In 1939 the government approved the construction of a defence battery at Waiheke, among other sites. It realised guns with a sufficiently long range installed at Stony Batter could protect the water from Cape Colville to Kawau Island. Another battery at Army Bay on the

Whangaparaoa Peninsula would protect the northern entrance to the gulf and provide safe anchorage for Allied ships.

Engineers designed tunnel systems unique to the contours of the land and 189 men were employed to dig the subterranean complex. A wharf was built at Man O'War Bay and connected to the site by a road, which carried vehicles bearing heavy machinery, sand and cement. The biggest problem during construction was maintaining secrecy – not an easy task when the gun barrels alone weighed 28 tonnes. The nearest power pole was (and still is) 5.5 km away, necessitating the use of generators to provide electricity.

The construction of 1 km of tunnels (each lined with 30 cm of concrete), three gun emplacements with associated underground magazines and explosives stores, control rooms, living quarters, engine rooms and a pump house was a logistical nightmare. In the meantime the war ended and the complex was never finished.

A bunkroom used by staff who manned the two guns that now serves as an exhibition room and display centre at the tunnels entrance. These is being painstakingly and comprehensively restored by the Stony Batter Protection and Restoration Society. The society was formed in 1999 to preserve and restore the site. This team of self-proclaimed 'dedicated nutters' has spent 18 months cleaning the tunnels and gun pits. When they first rediscovered the site after decades of neglect, the bottom tunnel was flooded calf deep and lay strewn with animal bones, sheep carcasses, glass, concrete, bricks and tree trunks.

At the entrance to the tunnels is the dead-end blast chamber, which has 1-m-thick concrete at the end wall. The tunnel turns left then right before continuing in the same direction. The system allowed a blast to be absorbed, preventing it from penetrating the tunnel system.

The first room is the magazine, which is approximately 24 m long, 8 m wide and 4 m high. It held 370 shells in three pyramidal stacks, separated with wooden guides like a wine rack. A steel rail around the top dangled a block and tackle that was used to move shells around the magazine. The shells, each weighing 172.5 kg, were hoisted up a shaft to the gun pit.

The explosive charge was detonated by cordite, which was stored in a separate room. The crew manning the store had to wear cotton clothes to avoid static electricity build-up and the possibility of explosion.

Off the bottom tunnel is the engine room, which housed two Ruston Hornsby diesel engines. These were the heart of the entire operation, supplying power to the guns, pumps and lights. After the pump room is a ladder to the gun pits.

The gun barrels were approximately 12 m long and nearly 1 m wide at the breach. The guns were the fifth biggest in the Commonwealth after examples in England, Canada, South Africa and Gibraltar.

The shells were loaded with two bags of cordite, each weighing 27.5 kg. The operators would shut the breach and fit the fuse, which was electrically fired. The obdurator sealed the barrel and stopped the backflash as the guns fired. For 14–16 seconds after firing, water and compressed air blasted through the barrel to cool down and blow out the gases through the muzzle. Turnaround between firing was normally 30 seconds, including changing the elevation. The guns had a range of 32 km.

There is no consensus on how many times the guns were fired, but they were never used in wartime. In the 1950s a gun was fired, and the percussion from the blast broke windows in Coromandel town, nearly 30 km away.

The fort was shut down at the end of 1957 when the coastal defence regiment was disbanded. In the 1960s the guns were chopped up and sold for scrap, with the plate steel being sold to Japan. The tunnels were left sealed but unprotected.

Coromandel

The western side of the Coromandel Peninsula borders the Hauraki Gulf, while the eastern coastline is brimming with golden sandy beaches enclosed by forest-covered headlands. Drowned river valleys with extensive estuaries and long sandspits have formed at Tairua and Pauanui.

Unusual rock formations and innumerable offshore islands around Cathedral Cove hint at a fiery volcanic past, a theme continued at the remote tip of the peninsula, discovered via the Coromandel Walkway.

16

Coromandel Walkway

This stretch of coastline along the north-eastern coast of the very tip of the Coromandel Peninsula offers dramatic views. The Coromandel Walkway forms the missing link in a 'loop' of the peninsula. It is well formed for its entire length and frequently signposted.

Grade	Medium
Time	7 hours return
Access	Stony Bay is 27 km from Colville and 9 km past Port Charles, at the roadend. Stock up on provisions at Colville. The start of the track is signposted from the carpark/kiosk next to the concrete ford at the Stony Bay campground. There are toilets at the DoC-administered campground. The other end of the walk starts from Fletcher Bay, a secluded bay with mature pohutukawa, 36 km from Colville and 7 km past Port Jackson. Follow the west coast to the roadend and DoC campground.

For the first 1¹/₂ hours from Stony Bay the coastal views are concealed by vigorously regenerating manuka and kanuka forest. The gentle gradient allows appreciation of birdsong made possible by DoC-implemented predator control. Bellbirds, tui and grey warblers bring the forest alive with their melodies. The dense stands of manuka and kanuka provide nursery conditions for pohuehue and ponga, while in the gullies nikau palm fronds form a canopy. For an appreciation of the coast, look for the 5-minute detour to a lookout. This gives a taste of what is to come.

The steep descent into and climb out of Poley Bay announce the coastal views. Sheer cliffs mottled with patches of tenacious vegetation fall to a rocky base and frothing white water. Great Barrier Island fills the northern horizon and Cuvier Island sits to the east.

At the base of the colourful cliffs, spire-shaped offshore stacks protrude from the agitated water. Fletcher Bay was the focus of volcanic activity on the Coromandel Peninsula around 18 million years ago. An andesitic volcano once dominated the area, its scant remains now forming Sugar Loaf Rock and the Pinnacles.

On the rocky shores below the track heading to Fletcher Bay are ancient trees resembling charcoal. Many millions of years ago the volcano spewed a river of lava, engulfing forests in its path. The incarcerated trees lay blackened and preserved in rock until exposure today through tectonic uplift and coastal erosion. The focus of volcanic activity later migrated south, leaving the Coromandel and the Kaimai Ranges in its wake.

The final section of the walk to Fletcher Bay traverses farmland and passes the Old Fencer's Hut. The dilapidated corrugated-iron shed and outhouse (with a view) are relics from early farming days. When large tracts of land were being fenced it was too far for the workers to return home, so rustic temporary accommodation was erected to provide shelter.

The walk is in the shadow of Mount Moehau (892 m) and Little Moehau, which are the two prominent landmarks at the northern end of the Coromandel Peninsula. It is said Tama Te Kapua, a notable commander of an Arawa canoe, lived and died near Moehau. Tradition instructed his whanau to preserve his remains in the hollow of a tree for one year. The body was then stripped to bone and his skeleton placed in a chest with his personal treasures. He was buried near the summit. On descending, one grandson said, 'He will have a windy sleep there.' Moehau thus took its name, meaning 'resting in the wind'.

Some Maori believe Moehau was once the domain of turehu or

patupaiarehe – little red men. They learned to survive in the misty conditions experienced on the mountain and collected water by distilling fog. When the bush is foggy and the wind whistles through the trees, their voices can still be heard.

The Moehau Range was formerly the stronghold of two native frog species. Neither Archey's frog nor Hochstetter's frog depend on ponds for breeding. Instead, the tadpoles grow into froglets within the egg. For their part, the adults receive moisture from rain, dew and mist. Recently a chytrid fungus has devastated the populations, with Archey's frog numbers down by 85%.

17

Whitianga Rock to Cooks Beach

This track explores part of the southern side of Mercury Bay, encompassing evidence of a Maori pa site, remnants of kauri logging, coastal views, beaches and important European history. Most of the walk is on an easy gradient and includes some beach walking.

Grade	Easy
Time	4 hours return
Access	From Whitianga, a passenger ferry crosses the mouth of the estuary continuously every day. The walk starts up the gravel track across the carpark from Ferry Landing on the Cooks Beach side and climbs the wooden steps.

Whitianga Pa was strategically located on top of the 24-m-high rock at the mouth of Whitianga Estuary. Ngati Hei, tangata whenua of the area, were the most likely inhabitants, but when Captain Cook visited in 1769, he saw only remains, suggesting the pa may already have been overthrown.

From the ditch behind the information board at the base of the hill the defences of the pa can be read like a story. The ditch was excavated to provide protection from attack and was probably fortified with a high wooden fence. A little higher, the terraced grass areas were probably the site of communal buildings and dwellings. Middens beside the track are the remains of shellfish on which the Maori fed. Postholes in the slippery rock once supported a wooden platform, the second line of defence should the ditch be breached.

From the summit of the rock (10 minutes to the top) retrace your steps to the information panel and traverse the defensive ditch to get to Back Bay. Tread carefully on the small rock platform at the base of the wooden steps, as this is lethally slippery. Expect to squelch through the swamp behind Back Bay. At low tide the remains of a boom used as a holding pen for kauri logs between the 1880s and 1910s can be seen near the mouth of the bay. Logs felled from the surrounding hillsides were trapped here before being transported to the mills on the opposite shore.

The soft rock of the cliffs above Back Bay has been hollowed by the wind into interesting patterns. Airborne sand and grit held aloft by the swirling wind has enlarged the holes to elevated caves.

The steep track now crosses the ridge (30 minutes) and can be slippery when wet. A large rock at the summit is the natural vantage point for a rest and a gaze up the Whitianga Estuary to the densely forested hills of the Coromandel Range. Descending to the road through dense groves of ponga, turn right and follow the track for 5 minutes to Flaxmill Bay. Below the road the creamy-white ignimbrite rock has been sculpted by waves and wind into bizarre, fluid mouldings. At low tide these can be explored from the exposed rock platform.

From Flaxmill Bay with its community of moored sailing vessels the white face of Shakespeare Cliff becomes evident. Some locals with lively imaginations can see the profile of an orator in the edge of the cliff. On his visit to Mercury Bay Captain Cook noted that this figure must be speaking poetry and named the feature after his country's most famous playwright. Other locals think Cook spent too long at sea.

From Flaxmill Bay the track perches by the cliff edge before crossing a grass paddock and meeting the vehicle track (30 minutes). In 1970 Queen Elizabeth II and her entourage visited the area to celebrate the bicentenary of Cook's visit and a royal picnic was held in the paddock.

The forest on the ascent has been replanted with kauri at the initiation of the Kauri 2000 Trust. This millennium project was set up in 1999 to restore the Coromandel's indigenous kauri forests. Over 13,000 trees have since been planted on the peninsula.

Head left along the metalled vehicle track to the summit carpark and walk the loop (3 minutes return). The two lookouts take in views of Mercury Bay. A plaque identifies notable landmarks and the sprinkling of islands decorating the bay. Below, Lonely Bay basks in splendid isolation and Cooks Beach stretches away in a golden arc.

Take care to watch for vehicles while descending to the carpark (10 minutes) and walk the short track to Lonely Bay. This charming beach is difficult to leave, especially when camped under the branch of a pohutukawa, listening to the soothing sound of wavelets fluttering to the shore.

To reach Cooks Beach takes a further 15 minutes. Climb to the carpark, descend to the sealed road and turn left. Take the signposted track that leads to the western end of the beach. Now is a good time for bare feet as it takes approximately 45 minutes of beach walking to reach the eastern end at Purangi River.

Near the eastern end of the beach a concrete rock cairn is not far from the spot where HMS *Endeavour* dropped anchor on 5 November 1769. Cook was able to establish cordial relations with local Maori and exchanged potatoes, nails and cloth for fish. He was impressed with the abundance of shellfish, including cockles, clams and mussels. He renamed the Purangi River as Oyster River on account of the delicious oysters he tasted.

One of the most noteworthy events of Captain Cook's visit occurred here on 9 November, when Cook and ship's astronomer Charles Green went ashore to observe the transit of Mercury across the face of the sun. By recording the time the transit began and ended, and with a sextant establishing the sun's altitude at the time of 'ingress', Cook and Green were able to calculate their longitude and latitude very accurately. Mercury Bay received its European name to commemorate this achievement, which allowed New Zealand to be positioned on the map in relation to the rest of the known world. Cook also decided to plant the English flag on a low hill to the far side of the Purangi River, thus claiming New Zealand for George III.

The Purangi Reserve at the mouth of the inviting Purangi River is a tranquil place to enjoy a picnic under the pines. Return to Whitianga via the same track, or cut out the section to Shakespeare Cliff by walking along the road.

18

Hahei walks

The coastline around Hahei, on the east coast of the Coromandel Peninsula, is among the most interesting in the North Island. Unusual rock formations, intimate scenery and marine reserve-protected waters enhance the atmosphere.

Cathedral Cove

Established in 1992, Te Whanganui-a-Hei Marine Reserve is managed by DoC to restore the rich and varied marine habitats that exist within its boundaries. Respect the information concerning restrictions posted on signs.

Grade	Easy
Time	1¹/₂–2 hours return
Access	Cathedral Cove is signposted along Grange Road from Hahei shops. The lookout carpark is at the top of the hill. Access to the track is also signposted from the northern end of Hahei Beach carpark (allow an extra 25 minutes each way).

There are few more memorable coastal views in the North Island than those from the lookout platform. The $80,000 platform was opened in 2001 and has interpretive panels on the lower deck introducing the region's geology and history.

The track to Cathedral Cove is one of the most popular walks in the region and receives a healthy maintenance budget from DoC. The surface is metalled and the detours to the delightful bays are comprehensively signposted.

After 10 minutes, the first side track will take you to Gemstone Bay, a pebble-strewn beach with a colourful cliff receding through the clear waters. Semi-precious stones such as jasper have been found here in the past. The next bay along, Stingray Bay, is sometimes visited by stingrays making the most of the protected waters of Te Whanganui-a-Hei Marine Reserve. While nearby Mares Leg Cove and Cathedral Cove are often busy, Stingray Bay is almost always refreshingly empty. The mesmerising patterns on the creamy-white cliffs to the north are a form of honeycomb weathering. Salt crystals deposited on the fine-grained ignimbrite rock expand when wet, levering it apart and loosening its structure. The small weakness is then enlarged by swirling winds to form a cavity. When many small hollows occur in close proximity the pattern resembles a honeycomb.

The track heads inland and climbs to a more open section of the track. Views span the Mercury Islands in the north to the Alderman Islands and Mayor Island in the south. The alternative route through the puriri grove is uneven but allows intimacy with the coastal forest of kawakawa and puriri. The puriri tree flowers year-round, and the pink blossoms are often scattered over the track like confetti. These gnarled trees are around 150 years old, and the hollows in their white bark are the home of the puriri moth.

Descending the wooden steps to Mares Leg Cove may require courtesy to the upcoming walkers. Mind your head on the low pohutukawa branches at the beach. A rock formation that resembled the hind leg of a horse used to jut from the southern headland but it collapsed after a storm in 1977. Toilet facilities are available near the rear of the beach at Mares Leg Cove.

The familiar image of Cathedral Cove has on many occasions been used to promote the Coromandel Peninsula, and Tourism New Zealand uses the natural rock arch in overseas advertising campaigns. Look up as you walk through the cavern: the crack in the ceiling is the weakness that has been exploited by the sea, which has been enlarging caves on both sides of the headland. In time this arch will collapse to form a stack such as the sail-shaped Te Hoho Rock at the northern end of Cathedral Cove.

Behind the beach tenacious pohutukawa trees cling to the glistening white cliffs, and their crimson blossom creates a striking contrast during early summer. The cliffs provide the parent material for the white sand below, which is tinged pink by ground-up scallop shells. The magical array of colours is completed by the blues of the water, which change with the weather.

Te Pare Historic Reserve

There are superb views of Hahei Beach from Te Pare Point, and in an easterly swell waves explode into foam on the offshore reefs. The walk through the reserve forms a gentle, short accompaniment to the Cathedral Cove walk.

Grade	Easy
Time	30 minutes return
Access	Entering the settlement of Hahei, take the first road on the right into Pa Road. The start of the track is signposted from the roadend. Alternatively, climb the wooden steps at the southern end of Hahei Beach.

The track is metalled as it crosses the long grass on the lower terraces of the pa. By the saddle in the headland, opposite the rocky bay, are the remains of a defensive ditch. Look also for the hollows that were used as food storage pits.

Hereheretaura Pa was inhabited by Ngati Hei. Their eponymous ancestor was the sail master Hei, who called out on sighting the beautiful coastline. He thought the curve of a headland on one of the offshore islands resembled the shape of his nose. The area was thus named

Te O-a-Hei, meaning 'the exclamation of Hei'. After burial at Hereheretaura Pa, Hei's bones were removed to Tokatea (Castle Rock). Viewed from the headland pa, the surf glows white as it cascades over the reefs of the offshore islands.

19

Tairua Harbour walks

These two walks explore the high points of the eastern coast of the Coromandel at the entrance to Tairua Harbour. The sandspit of Pauanui, the changing colours of the water in Tairua Harbour and the jagged formations of the inland range provide excellent views.

Pauanui trig

These walks can be combined to form a circuit of around 3 hours return. This description follows a route along Trig Track to the summit trig, descending via Cave Bay Track and returning along the coast.

Grade	Medium
Times	Trig Track 1¹/₄ hours one-way to trig Cave Bay Track 1¹/₂ hours one-way to trig Carpark to Cave Bay 20 minutes one-way Ocean View Loop Track 15 minutes return
Access	On entering Pauanui turn right into Pauanui Beach Road at the second roundabout. Where Pauanui Beach Road forks, take the left fork. The start of the walk is signposted

from the carpark at the end of Pauanui Beach Road. The parking area has toilets, benches and picnic tables.

Shortly after the start of the walk Ocean View Loop Track is signposted on the left. This 15-minute return walk is an easier option for those not wanting to attempt the complete circuit to the trig. It climbs gently through coastal forest and has benches from which to admire the views.

Continuing along Trig Track, take care over the steep and slippery sections. The track winds up through regenerating coastal forest diluted with mature self-seeded pines. Middens beside the track indicate Maori occupation of the high point, which commanded extensive views in all directions. The views would have differed vastly from today's, with the rampant development that has now taken over Pauanui and Tairua. The high density of holiday accommodation on the sandspit is indicative of the settlement's success as a destination and some of the 'baches' are among the most expensive in the North Island. The sandspit was formed from a series of around 60 parallel dune ridges, many of which have now been levelled through housing developments.

To return via the Cave Bay Track follow the signpost approximately 5 minutes below the summit. The potential slipperiness of the track is balanced by a more gentle gradient and a dense mat of pine needles coating the track surface.

Back at sea level, the return walk to the carpark via Cave Bay and Flat Rock follows the headland. Near the head of the bay is the wave-sculpted cavern that gives the bay its name. Enterprising locals have constructed a seat from which the cave entrance frames the coastal views. Flat Rock is a 'cobblestone' pavement formed from the weathering of columnar pillars of rhyolite lava. Wave action has smoothed the edges of the platform. The well-trodden pebbles at the top of the rocky beaches are the easiest walking surface to Flat Rock, from where the track is slightly raised from the foreshore and skirts the coastal forest.

Paku summit

Paku Hill is the emblem of Tairua and has featured on postage stamps. The eroded remains of the volcano are now covered in houses.

Grade	Easy
Time	45 minutes return
Access	From Tairua town centre follow Manaia Road for 1.2 km and turn right into Paku Drive. After 1.9 km veer sharp left and turn right into Tirinui Crescent. The start of the track is signposted from the end of the crescent 200 m farther on. If travelling to Tairua from the north, turn left into Ocean Beach Road before the one-lane bridge and continue 1.5 km before joining Paku Drive.

Paku Hill is a twin-peaked dome of rhyolite lava that was formed around 7 million years ago. It was formerly an entombed volcano, buried under an older cone that has since eroded away. The viscous lava didn't travel far before cooling and thus left a steep form. Paku was once an island but longshore drift has transported sand to join it to the mainland by the narrow neck of sand that closes off Tairua Harbour.

The track is steep and rocky in places as it zigzags up to the trig at the summit. There are extensive views of sediment-choked Tairua Harbour, up the Tairua River to the jagged pinnacles of the Coromandel Range. During the last Ice Age Tairua Harbour was a large river valley. Sea levels rose and huge quantities of debris were brought down from the ranges, choking the river system and forming the colourful patterns of sand seen on the estuary bed.

Bay of Plenty

White Island is at the centre of an arc which traces a sandy path through the Bay of Plenty. From the long sweeping beaches or the rare raised headlands, the plume of steam rising from the active volcano acts as a weather vane.

Coastal walks are confined to the occasional rocky points punctuating the otherwise sandy expanse and were also used by Maori, who were attracted to the coast by the abundance of shellfish and fish. The pa sites of Mount Maunganui, Bowentown Heads and Te Kohi Point at Whakatane give wide panoramas of the beaches and are replete with evidence of their settlement.

20

Orokawa Bay and Homunga Bay

This colourful coastline walk, north of the seaside resort of Waihi Beach, leads to the secluded, pohutukawa-fringed beaches of Orokawa Bay and Homunga Bay. These coastal gems can be reached only by foot, adding to their attraction.

Grade	Easy/Medium
Time	1^1/$_2$ hours return to Orokawa Bay 2^3/$_4$ hours return to Homunga Bay
Access	The start of the track is signposted from the northern end of Waihi Beach.

At high tide and in an easterly swell the advancing surf may mean scurrying between waves to avoid wet feet. The first section to Orokawa Bay rises up and over headlands along a well-formed track. If you are in doubt of the route, follow the arrows. Occasional pockets of coastal forest give some shade but from the exposed tips of the rocky headlands wide vistas of ocean stretch unbroken to the horizon. The first glimpse of Orokawa Bay is a treat, the scintillating golden sand enclosed by green headlands and an invitingly blue ocean.

From the far end of Orokawa Bay there is a 45-minute detour to William Wright Falls. The track crosses the narrow Orokawa Stream many times, but wet feet can be avoided with the convenient stepping stones. The falls cascade in two stages and are a cool shady spot for a rest on a hot day. Return by the same track to Orokawa Bay, where rustic toilets are provided.

The track from Orokawa to Homunga Bay is steeper and occasionally overgrown. Where the track crosses grassland, look carefully for the marker posts, some of which may be hidden under the long grass.

This section of coast feels raw and dramatic with the rhythmical pounding of the waves on the rocks below. The track leads through cuttings on the tops of the low cliffs, which have an unusual combination of colours left over from their volcanic past. Wind can accelerate through gaps in the cliff wall and this has contributed to some unusual formations in the rocks.

Homunga Bay is not as picturesque as Orokawa Bay, but has an undiscovered and isolated feel. Return to Waihi Beach via the same track.

21

Bowentown Heads

Bowentown Heads form the northern entrance to Tauranga Harbour. The remnant rhyolite dome is connected to the mainland by a sandspit stretching towards Waihi Beach. Maori exploited the high point in constructing pa sites.

Grade	Easy
Time	1¹/₂ hours return
Access	From SH2 follow signs along Athenree Road and at the beach turn right along Seaforth Road. The two carparks at Bowentown Heads are a further 5 km.

Bowentown Heads are the scant remains of rhyolite domes 5 million years old. The viscous lava formed steep-sided islands, although they have succumbed to millennia of erosion. Since the end of the last Ice Age and the stabilisation of sea levels around 6500 years ago, a long sandspit has connected the islands to the mainland.

The tracks at Bowentown are administered by Tauranga District Council. They traverse native coastal vegetation and scrub and are mostly on a grass surface. In places the thin soils have washed off to reveal the rock beneath. This can be lethally slippery when wet.

There are two points to the heads at Bowentown, explored from an upper and lower carpark. The upper carpark is closest to Te Ho Pa, the smaller of the two sites. This takes approximately 30 minutes return to explore. Head for the trig at the high point of the headland, which provides views right up the 11-km beach through Bowentown to Waihi Beach. To the south past Matakana Island are Mount Maunganui and the fading curve of the Bay of Plenty. Loop around the northern section of the hill to meet the road back to the carpark. Also departing from the upper carpark is a stepped track to Cave Bay, a sandy enclave at the mouth of the estuary.

Te Kura-a-maia Pa can be explored from both carparks. The significant terraces of the pa step between the two parking areas and a network of tracks overlays the grass. With its well-preserved form, Te Kura-a-maia is one of the most easily accessible pa in the region. The southern terraces were most likely the sites for dwellings, food storage pits and cooking areas. Large communal whare would have occupied the central area. The composition of middens reveals a diet dominated by fish and shellfish. As the pa was situated in a prime strategic location, guarding the mouth of Tauranga Harbour and with excellent access to food resources, it was often contested. It is thought to have originally been inhabited by Nga Marama, but Ngati Maru from the Hauraki Plains later occupied the site.

From the bottom carpark at Anzac Bay, follow the track from the northern end. The first 5 minutes are treacherously slippery when wet. At the crossroads the first two tracks on the left lead to a track that loops around the headland to Shelly Bay (10 minutes). Straight ahead also leads to Shelly Bay (5 minutes). From the far side of Shelly Bay continue along the track and climb to the summit of the headland by turning right at the fork after 5 minutes. The views here are land-oriented, with the Kaimai Range looming. To return to Anzac Bay head along the first track on the left.

22

Mount Maunganui walks

The extinct volcano of Mount Maunganui, also known as Mauao, is the great landmark of the low-lying coastal Bay of Plenty. The 232-m rhyolite dome erupted 4 million years ago and today stands sentinel over white-sand beaches and the massive expanse of Tauranga Harbour.

Base Track

The atmosphere and views change noticeably as the circuit around 'The Mount' is completed.

Grade	Easy
Time	45 minutes return
Access	The track starts from the northern end of Pilot Bay, or from behind the campground below Mount Maunganui.

The even track, administered by Tauranga District Council, is well frequented by locals and is popular with cyclists and joggers, who circumnavigate the volcano in quick time. It loops the base of the hill and is connected on the townward side by Adams Avenue.

Following the circuit clockwise from the bustle of the resort behind Mount Maunganui beach, with its high-rise apartments and lively café scene, the outlook changes to the industrial areas and the port of Tauranga. The estuary and city then give way to features less disturbed by humans, although Matakana Island is covered in exotic pine plantations. On the ocean side salty air accompanies the crashing of waves on the rocks.

The shade of the pohutukawa and whau is especially welcome during the Bay of Plenty's scorching summer days.

Summit Track

Being the undisputed high point of the region, the summit of Mount Maunganui has unparalleled views. City, beach, ocean and forested hills all fill the horizon.

Grade	Easy/Medium
Time	1¹/₂ hours return
Access	A 4WD track departs from the northern end of Pilot Bay. The steeper Oruahire Track starts behind the campground below Mount Maunganui.

A network of steep tracks leading to the summit weaves around Mount Maunganui. Take a few minutes to familiarise yourself with the track layout on the noticeboards at the start of the tracks, as navigation can sometimes be confusing.

Mount Maunganui is also named Mauao, which means 'trapped by the light'. One legend tells of three hills at the foot of the Kaimai Range. The beautiful hill Puwhenua was in love with Otanewainuku, a mighty hill nearby. A third hill was smitten by Puwhenua's beauty, but received only rejection because he was nameless. Distraught, he longed only to be cast into the sea to quash his worries. He asked the patupaiarehe (fairies) to help. One dark night the patupaiarehe dragged him to the coast, forming the Waimapu valley and Te Awanui (Tauranga Harbour). As the patupaiarehe could only appear at night, when the first fingers of dawn rose from the horizon they had to abandon the hill in his present resting place.

The easiest and quickest route to the summit is to take the wide metalled 4WD track from the northern end of Pilot Bay (45 minutes one-way). Another route via the Oruahire Track departs from the north-western end of Mount Maunganui beach and climbs via stone steps across pasture. After approximately 15 minutes there is a junction – left leads along Waikorere Track (20 minutes one-way to the summit) and right continues along Oruahire Track (30 minutes one-way to the summit). Waikorere Track is more challenging and climbs steeply, while Oruahire Track joins the 4WD track on the north-western side of the hill. If also attempting the Base Track, it is possible to join the Oruahire Track from an access track near North-west Rock.

23

Kohi Point Walkway

Startlingly clear remains of two pa, complemented by breathtaking coastal scenery, are the highlights of this Whakatane walk.

Grade	Easy/Medium
Time	3 hours one-way 7 hours return if continuing along Nga Tapuwae o Toi
Access	The walk starts up a set of concrete steps in Canning Place, 50 m from the junction with Commerce Street, Whakatane. Kapu-te-rangi Pa and the trig station can also be reached from the end of Kohi Point Lookout Road, off Otarawairere Road. There is access to Otarawairere Bay on a steep 45-minute (return) track from Otarawairere Road 1.3 km from the junction with West End Road in Ohope and 3.8 km from the start of Hillcrest Road in Whakatane. The Kohi Point section ends at West End Road in Ohope, where there are toilets. Nga Tapuwae o Toi returns to Whakatane via a loop that passes through coastal forest.
Notes	The rocks at the northern end of Otarawairere Bay are not negotiable around high tide. Check tide times at the Whakatane information centre before setting out.

The start of the walkway proper involves first climbing the concrete steps behind Pohaturoa Rock (the rock with the hole in Whakatane town centre) and continuing up Hillcrest Road on the footpath for 100 m. Look for the signpost on the right to Papaka Redoubt Historic Reserve, a 10-minute detour to views over Mount Tarawera, Whakatane, White Island and the Rangitaiki Plains to Mount Edgecumbe. The redoubt was constructed in 1869 for the armed constabulary during the time when Te Kooti's raids were most threatening.

To access Kohi Point Walkway, turn left opposite Papaka Redoubt Historic Reserve and go along Seaview Road for a further 200 m to the signpost on the left. The track follows a ridge above the town and after 5 minutes reaches a wooden footbridge and a lookout at the top of Wairere Falls. The first of the two pa is reached after a further 15 minutes. Kapu-te-rangi (kapu means 'reaching up to space' and te rangi means 'sky') Pa was also known as Toi's Pa and is said to have been occupied by Toi Te Huatahi. Many New Zealand tribes are descended from this notable chief, who originally came to New Zealand in search of his lost grandson, Whatonga. While competing in a regatta in his Polynesian homeland, Whatonga had been blown off course. Toi's search took him to Great Barrier Island, Coromandel Peninsula, Tuhua (Mayor Island) and eventually Whakatane, where he established the predecessor of today's pa.

Archaeologists have ascertained two distinct parts to the site, developed at different periods in its occupation. Oven stones found on the lower terraces beneath the track were used in hangi pits, probably before 1350. The main area of the pa was most likely occupied during the late eighteenth century and the long defensive ditches and banks were constructed to help ward off the frequent attackers keen to take over the strategic location. The pa may have been deserted for long periods over its history.

Shortly after Toi's Pa on the left, the track passes alongside the 250-m long defensive ditch of Taumata Kahawai Pa. The bank on the right is where the palisade fence would have been. Kumara pits near the side of the track are strikingly obvious. Houses and open meeting spaces were on the highest points, while cooking would have taken place on the lower terraces. This largest of the pa on Kohi Point was situated atop the steep slopes of the headland and afforded unencumbered views.

Fortified with a large defensive ditch and a heavily guarded central high point, the pa was virtually impregnable.

The track exits the forest and approaches a more open section with a low cover of flax. Views from Whale Island to White Island and Cape Runaway extend in a vast panorama. White Island's plume of steam varies in vigour and is an ominous indicator of geothermal activity in the region.

After approximately $2^{1}/_{4}$ hours the track drops into Otarawairere Bay, an isolated and secluded cove ideal for swimming. The rocks at the northern end of Otarawairere Bay are not negotiable around high tide. Pohutukawa branches provide shady spots for lunch. The track then continues to the carpark at West End Road in Ohope.

Either return via the same track, watching the tide at the rocky section to the north of the beach, or continue along Nga Tapuwae o Toi, a track that returns to Whakatane via an inland forested route. This 7-hour loop (including Kohi Point Walkway) is signposted from the base of the hill entering Ohope by road.

Eastland

Travelling clockwise along SH35 from Opotiki to Gisborne is like visiting a different country. The rugged topography, remoteness and sparsity of population give the district an undeveloped yet endearing feel. The land is full of surprises.

All walks on the East Coast are south of Hicks Bay. There are hidden stretches of golden sand such as Anaura Bay and Tolaga Bay, hemmed in by the exposed bluish-grey cliff faces of the characteristic papa rock. Captain Cook made his first forays into New Zealand waters here and documented his fascination at the new land.

24

East Cape lighthouse

The lighthouse at the tip of the East Cape near Te Araroa is a powerful place to watch the early fingers of dawn cast a misty tone over the parched tussock and manuka scrub. Flax leaves grate against each other with every breath of wind. In the distance below, rolling waves constantly caress – or pound – the shoreline.

Grade	Easy
Time	1 hour return
Access	From Te Araroa follow East Cape Road 21 km along the coastline to the roadend, where there is parking and toilets (although the doors may be locked). The start of the track is signposted 150 m before the carpark on the left.

The track climbs the cape steeply with the aid of handrails and several hundred steps. These wooden steps can be slippery when wet in the morning dew or the rain and the patches in between steps are sometimes muddy.

East Cape lighthouse, positioned at longitude 178 degrees 33 minutes east, is New Zealand's most easterly. The tower was constructed from cast-iron sections bolted together and is 14 m high. It has been on this site since 1922, having been removed from East Island after frequent landslides. It stands 154 m above sea level and the light flashes once every 10 seconds. The 1000-watt lamp is mains powered with a diesel generator for standby. Like all New Zealand lighthouses it is controlled by computer from Wellington.

25

Anaura Bay Walkway

The Eastland coast is studded with undiscovered beaches, many of which are remote and reached only via unsealed roads. Most headlands and coastal margins were stripped of native forest for grazing, leaving bare headlands with exposed grey papa rock tumbling to the ocean. Anaura Bay, tucked between Tokomaru Bay and Tolaga Bay, is a rare example of a beach flanked with pristine forest and accessible via a formal track.

Grade	Medium
Time	2 hours return
Access	From SH35, 14 km north of Tolaga Bay and 23 km south of Tokomaru Bay, turn into Anaura Road. Follow it to the beach, where it veers left and becomes unsealed. After it crosses a small creek there is a kiosk with an information panel. The walk starts from a stile opposite the campsite (no toilets and open only October–April).
Note	The track crosses private land and may periodically be closed. Seek local advice or contact DoC Gisborne before attempting the walk. There is no smoking along the route.

*Right: Algal film over white
ignimbrite rocks at Front
Beach, near Cooks Beach.*

*Below: From the summit of
Paku Hill views of Pauanui and
Tairua Harbour retreat to the
hills of the Coromandel Range.*

Above: The highest point of land in the area, Mount Maunganui has spectacular views in every direction.

Left: Secluded Otarawairere Bay can only be reached via the Kohi Point Walkway, adding to its appeal.

Right: A trip to remote East Cape lighthouse is best enjoyed at sunrise.

Top: The deserted golden sands of Anaura Bay are complemented by a rare remnant of Eastland forest in the recreation reserve. Above: The wharf at Tolaga Bay is reputed to be the longest in the Southern Hemisphere. Top right: Massive driftwood logs lie on the beach at the mouth of the Waikari River. Bottom right: Although famed for its gannet colony, Cape Kidnappers also has spectacular coastal scenery.

Left: Distinctive weathering patterns in the sandstone give Honeycomb Rock Walkway its name.

Right: Fur seals are relatively common around the southern coasts. Their smell usually gives away their presence.

Below: The wild seas around Cape Palliser give breathtaking displays of aquatic fury.

Above: The panoramic views from the gun emplacements at Makara are the reason the site was chosen for some of Wellington's World War II defences.

Left: Inspiring colours and uplifting scenery are the highlights of a walk beneath the White Cliffs.

The track is reasonably well formed, but single file for its length. For the first 25 minutes it skirts the forest, passing through streamside paddocks. Follow the posts and cross a stile into a narrow valley to the right.

The track arrives in a shaded stream catchment with steep banks. The vegetation is lush with green hues of ferns and lichens. Fantails flit cheerfully between perches and the echoes of bird call are everywhere. The forest is redolent with the calls of tui and bellbirds. Kereru flap in the puriri and kahikatea canopy. The track crosses the stream numerous times and is often wet and slippery.

After 30 minutes the track starts to climb out of the watershed, skirting pine forest. Cross a footbridge (10 minutes) and climb steeply through the pines. Take care following the marker posts, as occasionally the track becomes poorly formed through the long grass. Among the pines the occasional mature puriri stands out. On leaving the pines there are outstanding views of Anaura Bay's golden sands and Motuoroi Island.

On 20 October 1769 the view would have included the sight of Captain Cook's *Endeavour*. His name for the bay was Tegadoo Bay, possibly a misinterpretation of te ngaru, meaning 'the breakers'. To Maori it was known as Anaura. Immediately upon arrival *Endeavour* was surrounded by canoes filled with curious observers. Cook noted two men in distinctive dress and, assuming them to be chiefs, invited them aboard. Each was presented with four yards of linen. The Tahitian interpreter aboard explained that the nature of their visit was peaceful.

The following day Banks and Solander, the botanists aboard *Endeavour*, rowed ashore to collect plant specimens and 'to shoot some most beautiful birds'. They were escorted on a tour of houses and well-kept gardens where they noted the sweet potato, cocos (yams) and taro.

Dr Monkhouse, another scientist aboard *Endeavour*, made detailed observations of the village and examined the gardens, impressed that they were weed-free. He and the officers were treated to a substantial meal at which they were cordially welcomed by two chiefs after proffering beads as a gift. They ate lobster, which Banks noted weighed 11 lb, and were 'certainly the largest and the best I have ever eat'. Roots and bread accompanied the crayfish. In return for the hospitality, Dr Monkhouse passed round his brandy flask. To his surprise, the hosts seemed to enjoy the taste.

At the summit of the second ridge, where the breakers become audible, turn sharp right and descend the grass bank. The track enters native forest and then exits approximately 300 m farther up the road from the starting point. It is a welcome return from the forest to the coast, announced by the smell of the ocean and the percussion of the waves.

26

Tolaga Bay walks

The wharf at the southern end of Tolaga Bay is the township's major drawcard and is spectacular at any time of day. A trip up the northern headland is often overlooked but rewards with views of the tranquil Eastland bay.

Tolaga Bay wharf

The 660-m wharf at Tolaga Bay is reputed to be the longest in the southern hemisphere.

Grade	Easy
Time	30 minutes return
Access	Tolaga Bay wharf is situated at the southern end of the beach. From the township head south and turn left into Wharf Road, which leads to a parking area by the beach.

Tolaga Bay's wharf was completed in 1929 and served the busy coastal shipping route before the completion of the road to Gisborne. The road metal used in the construction of the main highway from Hicks Bay to

Gisborne was brought ashore at the wharf. After the road was finished coastal shipping declined, and thus the wharf contributed to its own obsolescence.

During the wharf's construction beach sand was used in the concrete. Its high salt content leached into percolating water, causing the reinforcing rods to expand and split the concrete, which now peels off like onion skin. A community initiative is underway to restore the wharf to its former glory. A walk along the old tramlines on the wharf allows admiration of the rock formations and strata on the adjacent cliff face. Under the wharf, bands of algae, molluscs and crustaceans encircle the pilings.

Tatarahake Cliff

Views down Tolaga Bay beach from the headland show it is sprinkled with driftwood, seaweed and other flotsam. Flanking the foreshore are low dunes covered with marram grass, and a line of Norfolk Island pines borders the road.

Grade	Easy
Time	30 minutes return
Access	Head north from the township and turn right into Forster Street. At the beach head left to the roadend carpark, from where the track is visible rising up the hill. There are toilets in the grass reserve between the dunes and the road.

The steep walk up the cliff face starts from the sign at the Tatarahake Cliff–Ernest Reeves Reserve and is aided by steps. It takes approximately 15 minutes to reach the lookout, which has views over the bay and inland to the pastured hills. The sheer exposed cliffs stretch out to sea, their bluish-grey papa rock mottled with occasional scraps of vegetation just holding on in a neverending battle with the sea.

27

Cooks Cove Walkway

Stunning views typical of Eastland scenery extend in all directions from the hills around Cooks Cove, near Tolaga Bay. Parched pastured hillsides cap exposed grey rock that protrudes into a deep blue ocean. The blue of the warm Eastland sky seems to distinguish this landscape from other coastal areas.

Grade	Easy/Medium
Time	$2^1/_2$ hours return
Access	From Tolaga Bay cross the bridge over the Uawa River and turn left into Wharf Road. After 1 km and a sharp left-hand bend, the grassed parking area is signposted on the right. The nearest public toilets are 300 m farther on, near the wharf.
Notes	The walkway is closed for lambing from 1 August to the start of Labour Weekend. No dogs are permitted.

The well-formed track climbs through manuka and kanuka before crossing a stile. Follow the marker posts over open farmland, cross another stile and continue to the wooden lookout (25 minutes). The lookout is 125 m above sea level and affords excellent views, especially on a fine day. The serenity of the small cove is immediately apparent.

The track descends through the shady canopy of kanuka forest via a winding route with steps, before reaching the flats behind Cooks Cove, where there are toilets.

Over the stile, turn left to the hole in the wall (5 minutes) or right to the monument (15 minutes) or continue to Cooks Cove and its northern headland (from the end of which glimpses of the Mitre Rocks appear).

The snug little bay was known to Maori as Opoutama and is nestled behind a headland just to the south of Tolaga Bay. Cook had heard from local fishermen that water and wood could be easily collected and Mitre Rocks (so named because they resembled a bishop's mitre) imparted shelter from the buffeting effect of the swell. He was also keen to establish some form of contact with Maori, as in previous encounters he had been met with wariness and hostility.

Captain Cook anchored here on 23 October 1769 and the following day, at high tide, came ashore for water and wood. The 'natives' were friendly and eager to trade. Trading occurred with fish being exchanged for cloth, beads and nails. Cook's men were able to load 12 tons of fresh water and three boatloads of wood.

On 25 October Cook rowed ashore and took several astronomical measurements of the sun and moon to determine his latitude and longitude. His armourer was able to set up a forge and repair the tiller braces. The well dug by Cook's men served to cool the iron worker's forge. It remained for over 100 years after Cook's visit and was named Te Wai-keri-a-Tepaea, and by later visitors as 'Cook's Well'.

Banks and Solander were able to make a foray ashore to collect plant specimens. Various botanical experiments were carried out including the boiling of manuka to make tea. A cabbage tree was chopped down and the cabbage apparently 'ate well boiled'. Bunches of scurvy grass were collected to aid the crew's health.

On one trip they encountered what Banks described as 'a most noble arch or cavern through the face of the rock'. To Maori this hole in the wall was known as Te Kotere-o-te-whenua and was used as a shortcut to commute between the two bays. Today the curious formation is still evident and offers remarkable views of Tolaga Bay through the opening. Strata of loosely bedded sandstone glow in the sun and the amplified sounds of the breakers echo through the cavern.

Nearby Pourewa Island was also explored by Banks and Spöring, who examined the prow and stern of a war canoe. They were equally impressed with the carving on a large house. After a successful and refreshing week at Cooks Cove, *Endeavour* weighed anchor at dawn on 29 October and headed north.

After exploring the sites of Cook's visit, return to the carpark via the same track.

Hawke's Bay

The region of Hawke's Bay is not renowned for its coastline. However, the first-time visitor will by pleasantly surprised by the rugged beauty of this majestic coastal stretch. Most coastal areas are at the end of long, winding unsealed roads and take some navigational skills to arrive at.

At the southern limit of Hawke Bay (the name given to the bay, not the region) are the dramatic cliffs of Cape Kidnappers and the resident Australasian gannets. Either side of Napier are lesser known coastal walks. The sandy excursion from Aramoana to Blackhead is a chance to witness the coastal fauna, while the dramatic and exposed coastal walks of Waikari and Waipapa are virtually unknown.

28

Waikari River and Waipapa Falls

These two tracks used to form part of the Hawke's Bay Coastal Walkway, which has been closed after active coastal erosion rendered sections of the beach impassable. Walked separately, they still give a good taste of the untamed scenery characteristic of this coastline.

Waikari River mouth

The beach at the Waikari River mouth is an exposed east-facing strip of coarse sand littered with detritus from the Waikari River.

Grade	Easy
Time	1 hour return
Access	58 km from Napier and 59 km from Wairoa along SH2, follow Waikare Road for 13 km to the signposted Waikari River Scenic Reserve. The unsealed road may be slippery and muddy after rain. There are basic toilets and a picnic area at the Waikari River Scenic Reserve.

The track starts from the stile behind the grassed parking area and follows orange markers along a narrow well-formed track (5 minutes). This meets a 4WD track that follows the true right (right hand side looking downstream) of the Waikari River until it drops to meet the beach.

Driftwood takes an assortment of shapes and forms, some of which would make the perfect perch for lunch or just to stop and watch the breakers cascade below the sheer cliffs. Goats graze the grassed slumps at the base of the cliffs and the salt-laden wind can howl up the cliff faces causing the slender grasses to dance in the wind.

Maori originally used the river mouth for landing waka and to access the river. From the 1860s onwards a bridle track followed the coastline. Mail was taken by horse to Gisborne along the coastal route, as valleys and ridges made an inland road impractical. The coastal route became obsolete in 1901 when a route via Tutira was completed.

In 1931, as a result of the earthquake that devastated Napier and Hastings, a huge slip known as the Moeangiangi Slip ripped a 3-km length off the 400-m cliffs. The slip can clearly be seen in the distant cliffs to the south of the beach.

Waipapa Falls

The pastel tones of the cliffs at the mouth of the Aropaoanui River look superb in storm or sun and the vast views to Bluff Hill and Cape Kidnappers provide memorable scenery.

Grade	Medium
Time	2 hours return
Access	29 km north of Napier and 88 km south of Wairoa along SH2, turn into Aropaoanui Road and follow it for 13 km. At the valley floor turn right and cross over two bridges. Access is through private property. The unsealed road may be slippery and muddy after rain.
Note	From time to time the track may become impassable because of erosion. Seek advice from DoC at Napier before attempting the walk.

The track surface varies between grass, sand, pebbles and boulders. After following the mouth of the Aropaoanui River it veers left along a wide but muddy grass track, occasionally crossing sand. As the track is flanked by open ocean on one side and bluffs that rise in a vertical wall for nearly 200 m on the other, it is difficult to stray.

After approximately 45 minutes sidle around the bluff by walking on the pebble- and boulder-strewn beach for 5 minutes, before rejoining the grass track to Waipapa Bay. This pebbled enclave surrounded by imposing cliffs is a delight and the 5-m Waipapa Falls disgorge into a swimming hole behind the beach. Watch for goats on the bluffs, which may dislodge stones onto the track below.

The rock on the cliff faces was laid down on the edge of a coastal shelf during the Miocene 20–25 million years ago. The muds and sands were compressed into the loosely bound rock seen today. Incorporated into the matrix is a vast array of fossilised cockles, oysters and fanshells, many strewn at the base of the cliffs. Cracked and partially visible examples sprout from the exposed rock face. Whether in loose rocks beside the track or in eroded specimens on the beach, there are fossils aplenty to be found here.

29

Cape Kidnappers Walkway

Cape Kidnappers, east of Hastings, is a coastal walk on a grand scale. The walk follows the beach all the way from Scotsmans Park at Clifton to the cape. Immense banded cliffs faulted to huge blocks form an impenetrable barrier on one side. The milky blue waters of Hawke Bay lap on the other. The area is famous for its Australasian gannets, which breed in colonies at the tip of the headland.

Grade	Medium
Time	6 hours return
Access	Cape Kidnappers is comprehensively signposted from SH2 in Napier and Hastings. The walk starts from the beach by the motor camp.
Notes	The walk is negotiable only around low tide. Leave no sooner than 3 hours after high tide and depart from the cape no later than 1¹/₂ hours after low tide. Even with this time window, wet feet may be unavoidable when clambering around rocks at the base of the cliffs. Seek tide times from local information centres. Access to the colony on the saddle is by permit only.

The sheer cliffs with their banded strata form a mesmerising adjunct to the walk. Interbedded layers of sediments read like a geological storybook and draw the eyes effortlessly along the headland. Some of the layers were deposited in shallow seas and exhibit occasional shellfish fossils. Other layers are freshwater in origin, a coarse conglomerate of pebbles and mud, while some strata are volcanic in origin, either ignimbrite or wind-blown ash and pumice. All were deposited between 300,000 and 1 million years ago.

The tilt and fragmentation of the layers is the result of upheavals caused by earthquakes. An apron of slumped material lies at the base of many faces and occasionally waterfalls pour from the tops. Watch for rock pigeons resting in holes and also the unusual weathering patterns in some of the layers. Despite the temptation to examine the rock, it is inadvisable to rest below the cliffs as rockfalls may occur. Take care also to avoid 4WDs and motorbikes, which use the beach as a highway.

It takes around 2 hours to reach the picnic shelter, where there are toilets. It is a further 30 minutes one-way to the plateau colony of gannets. The track departs from just behind the picnic shelter and climbs steeply over muddy paddocks and around a huge chasm by the DoC ranger's residence. Keep to the track as the cliff edge is nearby.

Cape Kidnappers is composed of papa rock, a bluish-grey siltstone formed 4–5 million years ago. It has been eroded to the shape seen today, with an impressive rock tower off the headland. Watch the waves crashing here and witness the immense height attained by the foam as it rises in slow motion.

Cape Kidnappers was given its European name by Captain Cook, who visited in 1769. After initial trading with local Maori, Cook's Tahitian interpreter was taken onto a waka against his will. In the ensuing altercation shots were fired, killing some Maori.

Cape Kidnappers has reached its fame because of its Australasian gannet (takapu) colonies. About 46,000 pairs breed around the New Zealand coastline, of which approximately 6500 pairs breed at Cape Kidnappers. Colonies were first recorded in 1870 by Henry Hill, a Hawke's Bay naturalist. He recorded 50 birds at the saddle colony. The plateau colony was established in the 1930s. Today gannets also breed around Black Reef.

The Australasian gannet is a member of the booby family. When chicks are four months old they undertake a 2300-km journey to Australia, returning to breed in New Zealand $2^1/_2$–$3^1/_2$ years later. They live over 20 years and mate with the same partner for life. They are expert fliers, often soaring and gliding on sea breezes. They can dive at speeds of up to 145 km/h and catch fish as much as 30 m below the surface. They inflate air sacs around their head and neck to cushion the impact and their nostrils are located internally to avoid water being forced into the nasal cavity.

The best viewing is at the plateau colony, where information panels describe their behaviour and life cycles. Heed all warnings concerning behaviour around the birds. Between July and January the gannets return to their original breeding grounds, establish partnerships, mate, nest and rear chicks. The close proximity of the viewing platforms allows observation of courtship displays, aggressive territorial squabbles (where beaks are locked amid much wing flapping) and rearing of nestlings. The updraught from the cliffs is harnessed by the birds to aid take-off. Watch them swoop and glide before deftly alighting on the hummocky terrain of their nesting grounds.

To return, follow the wide metalled 4WD track from the east of the plateau colony back to the beach.

30

Aramoana to Blackhead

The route follows a sandy beach south-east of Waipukurau and can be completed at all tides except high tide. It is best attempted at mid to low tide when the rock shelf is exposed and walking barefoot is possible.

Grade	Easy
Time	1¹/₂ hours return
Access	From Waipawa follow Pourerere Road to Pourerere through Taumumu and Omakere. Just before Pourerere turn right into Gibraltar Road and follow it 8 km to the roadend at Aramoana. To reach Blackhead from Waipukurau follow Porangahau Road then turn left into Wellington Road. Turn right into Tavistock Road, which becomes Farm Road. Keep left at the intersection with Middleton Road 6 km from the town. Where Farm Road leads to Motere Road keep left along Motere Road, which later becomes Long Range Road and leads all the way to Blackhead.

The eye-catching Aramoana homestead, on the hill behind the beach, is known as The Castle for obvious reasons. The three-storey weatherboard home with battlements around the parapets houses the sixth generation of the McHardy family. Along with the woolshed, it was built of Coromandel kauri in 1894. Landing boats on the notoriously choppy waters of Aramoana Beach proved trying for builders, who resorted to throwing the logs overboard and floating them ashore on the surf.

Aramoana beach is a perfect semi-circle of golden sand. Dunes, grassland and steep hills almost encircle the bay. The beach's arc has the effect of funnelling the waves, which break unevenly along the beach. This is a warning sign for would-be swimmers. Despite the appealing beach, the currents are dangerous, so seek local advice before entering the water.

The Te Angiangi Marine Reserve, established in 1997, covers 446 ha between Aramoana and Blackhead. Low tide exposes a subtidal rock platform, home to a variety of marine species including kina and paua. Large beds of Neptune's necklace, eel grass and coralline turf smother the rocks, and limpets encrust the surface. Greywacke rock falls to an undersea cliff face with kelp beds and rock crevices providing home to a large variety of fish and crustaceans.

Snorkelling and diving are popular activities and make the lengthy journey here more worthwhile. Locals are only too willing to advise of the best spots. A unique assemblage of fish species converges in the waters, as the East Cape current meets the cooler Southland current, providing an abundance of nutrients. The vast smorgasbord of fish attracts the occasional New Zealand fur seal to the beach. Although these creatures may seem tame, always remain landward and give them a wide berth.

It is a pleasant, easy stroll along the sand to Blackhead beach. Steep hills enclose the sandy beach, which has dangerous rips. Again, seek advice on the location of rips before swimming.

The rusticated woolshed hints at the main economy of Blackhead, only partially diluted with tourism in the summer months. There is a feeling of close-knit community among the faded baches. The campground toilets are for public use.

Wairarapa

The Wairarapa coastline is a savage place exposed to the wilds of the weather and ocean. The challenging conditions are complemented by an environment to match, with high cliffs tumbling to a narrow foot of flat land by the coast. When the winds are furious they conjure monstrous waves that unleash extravagant shows of foam.

At Castlepoint unique rock formations provide a sculptured backdrop to the walks. More unusual formations are also exhibited on the Honeycomb Rock Walking Track. Farther south at Cape Palliser the Wairarapa coast becomes wilder. Fur seals enjoy this coast and frequent the scattered rocks of the promontories on all the walks described here. Expect an encounter.

31

Castlepoint walks

From any angle the battlements of the reef at Castlepoint, east of Masterton, are fascinating. The unusual geology, charming lighthouse and small seaside community add to the enjoyment of this unique landscape.

Castle Point lighthouse

Castle Point is crowned by a 23-m lighthouse constructed of cast-iron sections bolted together.

Grade	Easy
Time	30 minutes return
Access	Access is from the carpark at the end of Jetty Road in Castlepoint. The settlement is signposted from Masterton. Follow Te Ore Ore Road from northbound SH2 in Masterton and continue for 64 km.

The track crosses a wooden footbridge over the neck of sand at the northern end of Deliverance Cove and climbs Castle Point on a concrete and wooden walkway. A boardwalk climbs to the summit and circles the lighthouse.

The lighthouse is sited 52 m above sea level and its light has a range of 26 nautical miles. The lighthouse was fully automated in 1985 and is controlled by computer from Wellington.

Watch for inquisitive yellow-eyed penguins around the rocks. The knee-high residents, blinking lazily while nodding their pinkish beaks, may be completely unnerved by human presence. Australasian gannets, black shags and white-fronted terns sometimes circle on the updraughts.

Deliverance Cove

Deliverance Cove is a delightful sheltered bay, perfect for swimming and relaxing after the walk.

Grade	Medium
Time	1¹/₂ hours return
Access	The start of the track is signposted from the carpark at the end of Jetty Road in the township of Castlepoint.

The track winds through pines above Deliverance Cove and exits onto a low ridge that circles the cove. The dunes are home to a rare and unique daisy – the Castle Point daisy *Brachyglottis compactus*, which grows only on The Reef and Castle Rock.

The Reef, which shelters Deliverance Cove from the breakers, is a jagged outcrop of fossil-rich limestone. Embryonic blowholes spout white water and seem to breathe with every wave. The Reef is very dangerous – heed warning signs about drownings before attempting any exploration.

The final climb up Castle Rock is very steep and the track narrows, but is well formed and easy to follow. Castle Rock reaches 126 m above sea level and was named by Captain Cook in 1770 because it resembled the turrets of a castle, with the reef presumably forming the battlements. The crumbling limestone overlies grey siltstone and is weathered to exotic forms. From the summit there are views north to the bulbous shape of

Deliverance Cove, resembling a fishing boat fender, and Castle Point. The coastline stretches in both directions to the distant horizon. Beware of freak gusts of wind, crouch low and keep well away from the edge.

To return, follow the well-formed narrow track down a spur at the base of the cliffs that exits at the southern end of Deliverance Cove. Watch for sunbathing fur seals. As ever, keep well away and stay on their landward side.

32

Honeycomb Rock Walkway

This is one of only a few coastal walks in the Wairarapa. The track, south-east of Masterton, passes unusual rock formations, a colony of fur seals and a rusting shipwreck.

Grade	Medium
Time	4 hours return
Access	From Masterton follow Gladstone Road 40 km to Te Wharau. Glenburn is signposted 26 km farther along a mostly unsealed road. The track starts from inside Glenburn station and is signposted on the left before the sign indicating the end of the public road.
Notes	The entire track crosses private land. It is closed from August to October for lambing. Please respect the property and keep to the marked track.

The track follows a narrow coastal strip at the foot of steep pasture-covered hills and is marked with orange triangles, some on marker posts. A windswept and rocky coastline stretches between jagged promontories and waves crash on shallow rocks just offshore.

Initially the track crosses a stile and heads through a paddock towards the sea. Through the gate it follows the fenceline, reaching a very boggy area before heading south.

For approximately 15 minutes the track follows a narrow grass strip between the rocky beach and paddock boundary. This is prone to erosion, so it may be necessary to walk along the beach. Smooth white pebbles flecked with grey adorn the beach and paua shells are abundant. After crossing another stile, head for the stile in the opposite corner of the paddock.

Although the track is marked with orange triangles, the raupo and wiwi here are so high they obscure the posts and in places the track is not well formed enough for the route to be found easily. Some muddy areas and a few wide streams mean heading to the beach periodically to avoid wet feet. However, the marker posts are never far away, so it's easy to return to the track.

The track continues to Honeycomb Rock, named for the weathering patterns in the 90 million-year-old sandstone. When sea spray soaks into the rocks, they become saturated with salt. As the water evaporates the salt crystals enlarge and lever the grains of sand apart. Wind then blows the grains in eddies to form the hollows. The pattern is best exhibited in overhangs where the face is protected from the rainfall.

A colony of fur seals inhabits the rocks near Honeycomb light (about half-way to Honeycomb Rock) and at Honeycomb Rock itself. They are camouflaged against the dark wave-beaten rocks. Take care not to disturb their sun-drenched slumber and always stay on their landward side.

Five minutes past Honeycomb Rock is the wreck of the *Tuvalu*, a Fijian trader that on 11 January 1967 ran aground on its maiden voyage. Rusting debris has been swept onto the shore during storms, and the main bow section still sits on the beach. There is little of interest past here. Return via the same track.

33

Cape Palliser lighthouse

The most southerly part of the North Island can be a savage place when buffeted by fierce winds and the accompanying sea swells. It is at its most invigorating during inclement weather, when the muted colours and misty spray make this place feel like the end of the earth.

Grade	Easy
Time	20 minutes return
Access	The drive to Cape Palliser is 37 km along Whatarangi Road, which is on the left before reaching Lake Ferry. The road is unsealed in places and towards the cape is severely threatened by active erosion. The ferocious power of the ocean is often witnessed at close quarters during the drive. There is a gravel parking area near the base of the steps to the lighthouse.

The 258 steps to the lighthouse replaced a steep slippery rocky path with a winch at the top. The lighthouse was established in 1897 and converted from oil to diesel generation in 1954. In 1967 it was converted to mains electricity. The tower is 18 m high and the cast-iron sections are bolted together. The light is 78 m above sea level. It flashes twice every 20 seconds and can be seen for 26 nautical miles. The 1000-watt lamp is controlled and monitored by a computer in Wellington.

The sounds of the wind and sea mingle in a duet that sums up this stretch of coast. Monstrous waves smash over offshore stacks in an orgy of foaming wrath. Enormous breakers crash on black shingle beaches and retreat in a maelstrom of white water. The wind picks up the exploding spray and bears it aloft.

The North Island's only breeding colony of fur seals has been at Cape Palliser since the 1990s. Fur seals (*Arctocephalus forsteri*) were hunted almost to extinction by the end of the nineteenth century, but numbers are now recovering. The bull seals at Cape Palliser organise territorial spacing by late spring. This is a battlesome affair and they don't eat or drink for about two months. The bulls, which can tip the scales at over 150 kg, sunbathe and rest on the rocks after feeding at sea. Keep on their landward side.

Seals are known as pinnipeds (wing footed) because of their webbed flippers. Streamlined bodies and blubber keep them warm. Their ears and nose are covered with flaps when they dive to feed on squid, octopus and hoki.

Wellington

The Wellington coastline forms the northern boundary of Cook Strait. Winds funnel through the gap between the North and South Islands, buffeting the hardy vegetation, which has evolved specialised communities around Makara and Pencarrow.

The rocky margins of land hide interesting geological histories, such as those at Turakirae Head. Any exploration of this coast is guaranteed to blow the cobwebs away and leave you marvelling at Nature's forces.

34

Turakirae Head

The raised beaches inland from Turakirae Head, at the western end of Palliser Bay, are reminders of the Wellington region's precarious tectonic stability. Successive earthquakes have formed raised tiers encrusted in vegetation and bordered by a restless sea.

Grade	Easy
Time	2 hours return
Access	From Wainuiomata follow Wainuiomata Coast Road to a metalled parking bay on the right near the coastline. The start of the track is signposted.

Follow the road from the carpark until it enters Orongorongo station, passing through a gate after 15 minutes. This is private land with a covenant allowing it to be crossed, so stay on the seaward side of the fence. The track is composed of pebbles and is wide and well formed. Follow the fenceline and cross another stile.

The route enters Turakirae Head Scientific Reserve. The unmistakable smell of the resident fur seals wafts on the breeze. Watch for their slumbering forms camouflaged against the rocks, or the patches of rock stained by the rubbing of oily bodies.

The vegetation includes flax, divaricating pohuehue, and toetoe protruding through beds of raupo. The greys of lichen-covered rocks are complemented by the mute greens of flax leaves.

In 1855 one of the most severe earthquakes in recent history elevated the area between Wellington and Palliser Bay by over a metre, and other upheavals are remembered in pre-European history. Several other occasions over the last 7000 years have been noted by geologists.

Each uplift has raised the beach so the area around Turakirae Head is now a series of beach terraces. From ground level they look like the creation of relentless waves pushing gravel up to the high-tide mark, but geologists have ascertained that the gravel beaches were uplifted almost instantaneously during the earthquakes. The beach closest to the hills, now smothered by scree, is thought to have formed around 7000 years ago. It was lifted another 3 m about 6000 years ago. A thousand years later an elevation of 6 m formed the next beach down, then around 3000 years ago there was a further uplift of 9 m. Maori oral history tells of the Haowhenua earthquake about 500 years ago, which raised the fourth beach. Closest to the sea the fifth beach was raised 2.5 m by the 1855 quake. While walking to the head, look to the left to the tiered profile of the beaches. Between each ridge the rocky areas would have been part of the intertidal zone before successive uplift by tectonic forces.

Radiocarbon dating has been the most reliable method used to determine the dates of the events. Analysis of core samples taken from behind the oldest and highest beach have uncovered remains of trees, freshwater shells and fur seals.

Return via the same track.

35

Pencarrow Head

This walk skirts the hills around Pencarrow Head from the entrance of Wellington Harbour to Cook Strait. It is a gradual transition from the seclusion and urban feel of the harbour to the uplifting, exposed coast.

Grade	Medium
Time	3¹/₂ hours one-way
Access	From SH2 at Petone follow The Esplanade to Waione Street and cross the Hutt River. Turn right into Seaview Road, which runs into Eastern Bays Marine Drive. At Eastbourne this runs into Muritai Road, which reaches the roadend at Burdans Gate. There is a parking area with picnic tables and toilets.
	If starting from Barings Beach, from Lower Hutt follow signs to Wainuiomata Road over the hill. After Wainuiomata the road leads through the Wainuiomata valley to Orongorongo. There is a carpark at Barings Beach but no toilets.
	If attempting the walk in one direction only, arrange to have transport at the walk's conclusion as there is no public transport.

Notes The Wainuiomata River mouth, which is sometimes knee deep, may need negotiation. Seek advice on the river level before attempting the walk. On Barings Beach watch for 4WDs, mountain bikes and occasional quarrying trucks. The winds along the walk can be very strong.

From Burdans Gate pass through the gate and follow the wide metalled road for approximately 1½ hours to just below Pencarrow Head. This is the least interesting section of the walk, with steep gorse-covered hills and occasional gullies of ngaio on the landward side. Watch the ferries navigate the entrance to Wellington Harbour and the aeroplanes jostle with the wind on their approach to the runway.

A signpost on the left marks the steep track up to the old lighthouse. The track passes the fenced grave of Evelyn Violet Amy Wood, the daughter of one of the lighthouse keepers. She died in 1896. The lighthouse was the first in New Zealand and operated from 1 January 1859. In 1906 the lower Pencarrow lighthouse was built, and it still operates today. There are good views from the upper lighthouse, from Wellington Harbour along the horizon south to Mount Tapuae-o-Uenuku (2885 m) and the Inland Kaikoura Range.

Orange circles on posts indicate the alternative descent track that exits at the mouth of Lake Kohangapiripiri. This detour takes approximately 30 minutes. Lake Kohangapiripiri is one of two inland lakes that occupy a valley formerly drowned by the sea. They became narrow sea inlets around 700 years ago when spits formed to isolate them. In the last 1000 years continuous gravel bars have built up and been widened by successive earthquakes. An alternative route inland is signposted from the eastern shores of Lake Kohangapiripiri, taking a route around Lake Kohangatera.

Continue along the road for 30 minutes past Lake Kohangatera and the wreck of SS *Paiaka*, which rests solemnly on the roadside. One of 40 ships wrecked along this coast, she was launched in 1881 and met her end in 1906. At Baring Head waves thunder onto the rocks in cataclysms of spray held aloft by the ever-present wind. Fields of kelp glitter like swarms of eels and orange lichens adorn the rock.

The gravels along this stretch of coast harbour a raised beach plant community. *Pimelea urvilleana* is a cushion plant composed of snaking accretions of spongy dark-green leaflets. *Raoulia hookeri* forms a mat of triangular pale-green leaflets. Both withstand the harsh winds, salt spray and severe desiccation. Sand buttercup and horokaka (ice plant) are also prevalent.

Endemic moths breed on the cushion plants, as does a rare species of dragonfly. These communities are so unusual that they probably contain still unnamed species. Banded dotterels and variable oystercatchers nest on the gravel between August and January, laying camouflaged eggs.

The road continues to Baring Head for another hour, after which it is necessary to walk on the large pebbles of Barings Beach for a further 30 minutes to reach the carpark. Barings Beach is a remote and raw stretch of coast that will blow the cobwebs away. The Wainuiomata River mouth, which is sometimes knee deep, will need to be crossed.

36

Makara Walkway

In World War II fortifications on high points around Wellington were part of the city's defence strategy. The now decayed gun emplacements near Makara naturally still boast the elevated viewpoint that made this spot on the west coast a preferred location for armaments.

Grade	Medium
Time	3 hours return
Access	The track starts from the west end of Makara Beach at the end of Makara Beach Road, where there are toilets.
Note	The inland section of the track is closed for lambing between 1 August and 31 October.

Makara Beach is a desolate place that funnels wind from the west up the gully behind it. The beach and settlement are not without their charm, as the bach owners to the north have tiny shacks at the foot of the sheer cliffs. Before embarking on the walk, examine the Makara Foreshore Reserve at the eastern end of the beach, a fenced area housing a regionally rare sample of indigenous coastal plants. Two plants of note include *Pimelea*, a cord of spongy dark green leaflets, and *Raoulia*, a mat of triangular pale green leaflets. Both hug the ground to avoid the wind, salt desiccation and sand blasting of the harsh environment.

For 10 minutes the track follows the coast until it reaches a signpost. From here the track is marked with occasional yellow-banded posts. Heading left up the hill to the gun emplacement takes approximately 40 minutes. The track is very steep until it meets the ridgetop, from where it undulates up the ridge following the fenceline. Beware of strong updraughts from the sheer cliffs to the right.

It is easy to understand why the 73rd Heavy Battery under the 10th Coast Regiment chose this site for gun emplacements. The views north stretching past Mana Island and the Marlborough Sounds seem close enough to touch. The guns were manned between July 1941 and February 1943, then removed in June 1944. The concrete structures and pedestal housing for the two 6-inch guns are still evident and the semicircular opening where the barrels pointed gives a good indication of their possible target areas. The lookout at the top of the hill and the foundations of the other service buildings, a little inland from the track, are also worth exploring.

The track then follows marker posts for 10 minutes before dropping down a signposted metalled road through a gully to Opau Bay (30 minutes).

To follow the rocky coastline back to Makara takes $1^{1}/_{2}$ hours. The second headland after $1^{1}/_{4}$ hours' walking requires boulder hopping to traverse. Use the well-trodden track at the top of the beach to make travelling over the loose rocks and pebbles easier. The beach is great for beachcombing through driftwood, seaweed and shrapnel of paua shells. Look for white-fronted terns, kingfishers, black shags, New Zealand pipits and the ubiquitous black-backed and red-billed gulls.

Wanganui, Taranaki and Waikato

The Wanganui coast, a sweeping expanse of sandy beaches bordered by dune fields and low plains, is occasionally punctuated by rocky promontories and river mouths. There are few easily accessible coastal walks, although the one stand-out is the walk from Castlecliff to Mowhanau Beach.

The Taranaki coastline follows the arcing contour of Mount Taranaki's base, exposing it to wind and waves from all directions. The black sands and rock outcrops create a unique character.

Farther north, the coast of the Waikato has a wild feel. It is open to prevailing westerly winds and is the first land moisture-laden winds reach on their journey across the Tasman. In these conditions the scenery comes into its own.

37

Castlecliff to Mowhanau Beach

The colours on this stretch of the Wanganui coast are striking in any weather. In overcast conditions the sand and cliffs have muted pastel shades, while in the glow of the sun there are marked contrasts in tones.

Grade	Easy
Time	2 hours one-way
Access	The walk starts at the beach domain at Castlecliff, a suburb of Wanganui. Access to Mowhanau Beach is along Kai Iwi Valley Road, 15 km west of Wanganui, or along Maxwell Station Road if coming from the west.
Notes	This walk is best attempted one-way, so arrange transport at Mowhanau Beach. Near Mowhanau Beach the cliffs protrude into the sea and are negotiable only when the water level is low. Aim to arrive at Mowhanau Beach close to low tide.

Castlecliff is the most southerly black-sand beach on the west coast of the North Island. The outflow of the Whanganui River discharges vast quantities of wood from its extensive catchment area in Whanganui National Park, and the beach sometimes resembles a raft. Driftwood of all sizes chokes the beach after storms, and locals take advantage of the free firewood by loading trailers near the rock wall at the southern end of the beach. The local council employs a bulldozer to shift wood to either end of the beach. This seems to be a perpetual operation.

According to Maori legend the Whanganui River formed after a battle between Mount Taranaki and Mount Tongariro, both in love with the beautiful Mount Pihanga. Having admitted defeat, Mount Taranaki fled the central North Island battle site, travelling west and leaving a deep wound in the land on his journey towards the sea. When Tongariro healed the wound left by Taranaki, the scar formed the Whanganui River.

Kupe, the great early Polynesian explorer, made landfall at Castlecliff. He named it 'Kai-hau-o-Kupe' – the place where Kupe ate nothing but wind. Although most of Kupe's exploration was around the coastline, he ventured up the Whanganui River.

The walk follows the coastline from the northern end of the beach along the base of the cliffs. The grey papa rock is composed of compacted mud and has slumped to create a blocky apron at the base of the cliffs. After enduring the ravages of the sea, these blocks are ground down to smaller rockeries of smooth stone encrusted with thousands of tiny mussels. Views follow the cliff line north to Wainui, nearly 10 km away.

It's around 2 hours to Mowhanau Beach, the first significant break in the cliffs. The black sand changes hue with the light, at times jet black, at others the colour of eggplant. The beach was known as Kai Iwi, but the name has been changed to avoid confusion with the nearby settlement of the same name.

Alexander's Redoubt on the southern hills above the beach was used during the New Zealand Wars in the 1860s and was one of the main fortifications defending Wanganui. Little evidence of it remains today. More recent World War II defences on the cliff were deliberately pushed off because erosion threatened the safety of the structure. Their remains lie at the mouth of the Mowhanau Stream.

There is a 20-minute return walk north along the beach. After 5 minutes an elaborate footbridge crosses Kai Iwi Stream, where birds take advantage of the nutrients at the mouth of the stream. White-faced herons and pied shags search for prey and rock pigeons flit in and out of roosting holes in the low cliffs. Kingfishers dart above the lagoon and gannets feed out at sea.

Follow the path up the hill. On the descent along the road back to Mowhanau, look up to the southern headland to the remains of the Old Coach Road. This formed a section of the Cobb & Co. coach service between Wanganui and New Plymouth, which in turn linked Wanganui with the major northern settlements. The inaugural journey took place on 11 January 1871. From Wanganui the coaches headed inland to Rapanui, where horses were changed, then descended to the beach at Mowhanau and followed the coast to Okehu. The journey to New Plymouth usually took two days.

38

Opunake Walkway

Part of the attraction of this walk is its varied terrain and scenery. The walk traverses farmland, coastal boulders and sandy bays. It is a showcase for the proud community of Opunake, South Taranaki, who have worked hard on the upkeep of their facilities and attractions.

Grade	Easy
Time	2¹/₂ hours return
Access	There are numerous places to join the track. A good place to start is from the carpark on Layard Street off SH45. Maps of Opunake Walkway are posted at Layard Street carpark, Dieffenbach Street and Halse Place, but track markers are sparse. Toilets are situated at Layard Street, the beach and the cemetery off Halse Place.

The carpark in Layard Street is by Opunake Lake, which was created in 1921 by the local electricity company to feed the power station under the cliffs at the eastern end of the beach. Occasionally a siren sounds when the lake is about to discharge water into the bay.

Follow Park Place past the constabulary cemetery on the left, and shortly after climb the stile on the right. For the first 15 minutes the track crosses paddocks over fences (some of them electrified!). Although poorly marked and not well trodden, the track basically follows the western side of the Waiaua River to the coast. Follow the gravel road along the coastline (15 minutes) until returning to the Layard Street carpark.

The next section of the walk descends the steps to Opunake Beach from the grassy area opposite the carpark. It is a fine, sheltered cove, immaculately kept and picturesque from every angle. The beach pavilion was built in 1931 and originally functioned as a tea room. Walk west along the beach to another set of steps at the far end.

The remains of the old wharf are visible from the headland at the western end of the beach. During the late 1800s Opunake tried hard to promote itself as the premier port of Taranaki by constructing a wharf on the western headland of the beach. The Tasman Sea's furious storms destroyed the wharf, so the town built a second jetty, the remains of which are still visible today. But unloading cargo such as flax was notoriously difficult in the choppy water and New Plymouth gained favour and developed into the main commercial centre of Taranaki. Opunake was left to become the quiet and charming surfers' hangout it is today.

Above the beach is an old shipping marker made from four slabs of totara bolted together. Ships aiming for the wharf could line up this marker with another at the beach pavilion to aid their approach.

Follow the grassed areas to a gate opposite Allison Street and cross the overgrown paddock. The track drops in and out of a small gully, with a wooden footbridge to aid the crossing of the creek. Follow the fenceline and small river valley to the coast once again. This rounds the headland to an elevated wooden lookout constructed by the Lions Club. From each of the headlands there are vistas along the coastline with low stratified cliffs undulating between bays. This section of the walk to Middleton Bay takes 30 minutes one-way. Middleton Bay, although less aesthetically appealing than the beach at Opunake, still has a certain charm, hemmed by sheer cliffs and surrounded by native vegetation.

The next section of the walk is tidal. The high-tide route uses a grass track between two paddocks. From the gravel carpark at the Lions Lookout follow the grass reserves above Middleton Bay. On the western side of the bay a short detour arrives at another wooden lookout. Carrying on alongside the cemetery reaches Te Namu Pa. This section of the walk takes 20 minutes one-way. To reach the pa requires getting wet feet or disobeying the 'Bridge Closed' sign on the rusting beam over the creek.

Return via the mid- to low-tide route, which follows a coastal section around the headland between Te Namu Pa and Middleton Bay. From Te Namu Pa follow the eastern side of Otahi Stream to the river mouth and boulder hop around the headland (approximately 15 minutes). Walk along Middleton Bay to the toilets at the eastern end and climb the steps to rejoin the walkway.

To return take a shortcut via Dieffenbach Street, which cuts out the section to the lookout. Bowen Crescent and Fox Street also return to the Layard Street carpark.

39

Paritutu Rock

The impressive pinnacle of Paritutu Rock, New Plymouth, is actually a volcanic plug. This walk is more of a climb and should not be attempted by those with tendencies to vertigo.

Grade	Hard
Time	30 minutes return
Access	To access the start of the track head for the parking area near Paritutu Road off Centennial Drive. From central New Plymouth head west along St Aubyn Street, which merges with Breakwater Road. Turn left into Ngamotu Road and immediately right into Centennial Drive. The parking area is on the right. If coming from the west follow Beach Road from Omata until it becomes Centennial Drive.
Note	This climb is not for the faint-hearted. Confidence at height, all four limbs and good flexibility are essential.

The track at Paritutu Rock is extremely steep and slippery but the ascent is aided by a cable bolted into the rocks. The surface has been worn smooth by numerous footfalls and it can be difficult to find purchase. The lack of good foot and hand holds means large steps often have to be taken. The narrow gullies have been filled with hard-trodden mud. Watch for other climbers and look out for good places to pass them.

Paritutu Rock is an eroded andesite dome that was disgorged around 1.75 million years ago. It stands sentinel over the 749-ha Sugar Loaf Islands Marine Protected Area, which was established in 1991. The area was selected for protection because of the abundance of aquatic and terrestrial life. The islands harbour over 86 native plant species, and 80 recorded fish species inhabit the fertile waters. Fur seals also breed on Whareumu.

Most of the islands have been occupied by Te Ati Awa and Taranaki tribes. The area was on the fringe of agreed land boundaries and there were many territorial disputes. People of Te Ati Awa, following their defeat of Waikato tribes at Otaka Pa in 1832, moved to Moturoa and Mikotahi Islands.

They were named the Sugar Loaf Islands by Captain Cook in 1770, as they reminded him of the way sugar was stored in heaps or loaves. European whalers and traders lived on the islands from 1828. Following the construction of Port Taranaki in 1881, reclamation and the building of the breakwater joined Mikotahi to the mainland.

Port Taranaki and all its workings dominate the view to the north. Massive oil tankers and cargo vessels seem like toys from the summit but the chimney of the New Plymouth power station stands alongside like a lesser twin of Paritutu.

The city of New Plymouth and fertile paddocks stretch into the distance to the south. Back Beach, a fine stretch of sand barricaded by sheer cliffs of orange sandstone, sweeps along the coast. As this is Taranaki, the mountain is always there, except when low cloud hides its upper reaches.

40

White Cliffs Walkway

Unrivalled cliff formations border the coastal section of the walk and mesmerise the senses with colours, textures and patterns. This stretch of untamed coast between Urenui and Mokau is testimony to the relationship between land and sea.

Grade	Medium
Time	4 hours return
Access	6.7 km north-east of Urenui, turn into Pukearuhe Road and follow it to the roadend. The start of the walkway is signposted up the farm track towards the river mouth. Parking is on the roadside near the bridge.
Notes	The beach section at the base of the White Cliffs is only negotiable 2 hours either side of low tide. Plan your walk accordingly. The walkway is closed for lambing between 1 July and 30 September.

The hill on the left at the start of the walkway housed Pukearuhe, a near-impregnable Ngati Tama pa. Along with Ngati Mutunga, also part of the Te Ati Awa confederation of tribes, Ngati Tama withstood attacks for centuries. The pa was bounded on the seaward side by 100-m cliffs falling to a tumultuous sea, with a steep-sided barricade sloping down to Waikaramarama Stream, and a swampy stream on its western face. It was virtually untakeable when fortified with palisades and embankments. It was only when the northern tribes attacked in the early 1800s with muskets gained from trade with whalers that the defences were finally overcome.

Before the advent of Europeans the main route of the northern tribes on their raiding forays to Taranaki was along the coastline. At Waikaramarama Stream they were forced inland by the sheer cliffs and funnelled beside the pa, making them easy prey. The inland route was impenetrable, with steep hills cloaked in dense forest.

Cross the stile and head up the farm track for 45 minutes over private farmland. On reaching a grassy plateau surrounded by vegetated papa cliffs, it is a little tricky to spot the next stiles. Look to head left to the low point in the ridge below Mount Davidson (286 m).

The track cuts through the forest of White Cliffs Conservation Area. Access was made possible by the construction of the gas pipeline, and occasional marker posts show its subterranean location. The final drop into the basin of Waipingau Stream is aided by hundreds of wooden steps.

At the junction cross the swingbridge to complete a longer route via Waikorora Stream (add $2^1/_2$ hours) or turn left and follow Waipingau Stream for 30 minutes to the beach. This track can be wet and muddy. Beware of violent winds funnelling through the gap in the cliffs at the mouth of the stream. Turn left and follow the beach below Whitecliffs for 1 hour to return to Pukearuhe Road.

The White Cliffs tell a geological story with their colourful banded strata and boulders strewn at their base. The mudstone was deposited at the mouth of a river and settled into distinct layers. During stormy episodes, when the energy of the water hurtling down the river was enough to move boulders, these too were transported to the river mouth, where they settled. Boulders and sediment accumulated and compacted in layers over millennia, only to be lifted up and exposed by tectonic movements.

Today relentless gnawing by the waves eats at the soft mudstone, causing slabs to collapse, caverns to be excavated and weaknesses to be incised into crevices. The boulders released from sedimentary entrapment fall to the base of the cliffs and provide the scattered displays on show today.

When a showery westerly buffets this coast the cliffs become smothered in a light sheen. Breaks in the clouds allow sunlight to penetrate and illuminate the cliffs' palette of vibrant colours. An algal film in some layers adds green to the grey, terracotta, orange and ochre strata, and paints a striking canvas.

41

Waikawau Beach

The beach at Waikawau, between Awakino and Marokopa, is a hidden gem of the Waikato coast. The stock tunnel forms a unique entrance corridor to the black sands and deeply eroded cliffs of the beach.

Grade	Easy
Time	45 minutes return
Access	Waikawau Beach Road is 33 km from Awakino and 33 km from Marokopa. From Awakino follow Manganui Road, which is 2 km east of the town. From Marokopa follow Mangatoa Road. The winding road is only partly sealed and passes through native forest, pine plantations and farmland. Waikawau Beach is 5 km along the unsealed Waikawau Beach Road. This is very narrow with extremely tight corners through the road cuttings. Look out for wandering stock and oncoming vehicles. There is a parking area and toilet at the tunnel.

In the carpark it is easy to wonder where the beach is, as it is shielded behind high hills. The smell of the sea hangs on the breeze, but the ocean is still distant. The 50-m disused stock tunnel is a fitting entrance

159

to Waikawau Beach. From the first step, the echoes of waves breaking reverberate around the tunnel and announce the nearby sea. The light at the end of the tunnel is too hazy at first to make out details, but nearing the exit the sight of rolling waves and the expanse of black sand inspires a quickening of the step. At the mouth of the tunnel it is like entering a different world.

The tunnel was constructed with picks and shovels by Jim Richard Scott, Charlie Christofferson and Bert Perrett, all employees of the government works department. It was excavated to open up the beach route for stock to reach the 4000-ha Nukuhakari station, and was designed to be wide enough for the widest horned beast and tall enough for the tallest horseman. The construction was a point of interest for early settlers, whose children would play in the dark recesses, accompanied by the smell of dung and the sound of water dripping. Today the floor can be wet but is usually passable without getting feet too dirty.

Around the wild and dramatic beach, tufts of flax cling to the sheer faces of the sandstone cliffs. Closer examination of the loose rock structure reveals it is etched with lines and hollows – weaker strata exploited by wind and water. Views north of the tunnel retreat to misty headlands shrouded in a gauze of sea spray. After periods of rain, waterfalls pour over the cliffs. These are a warning to pay attention to possible rock falls from the cliffs. An exploration south of the tunnel encounters numerous sea caves.

This is a truly isolated and awe-inspiring beach, characteristic of the west coast's uplifting nature. It is a deserving reward for the effort to reach it.